# I
# AM
# A MOB
# BOSS

# I

# AM

# A MOB

# BOSS

## THE LAST CONFESSION
## OF A CRIMINAL KINGPIN

ANONYMOUS

WELBECK

The right of Anonymous author to be identified as the Author of
the Work has been asserted by them in accordance with the
Copyright, Designs and Patents Act 1988.

First published in 2025 by Headline Welbeck Non-Fiction
An imprint of Headline Publishing Group Limited

1

Cataloguing in Publication Data is available from the British Library

Paperback ISBN 978 1 0354 2619 5
eBook ISBN 978 1 0354 2620 1

Typeset in 11/18pt Adobe Garamond Pro by Jouve (UK), Milton Keynes

Printed and bound in Great Britain by Clays Ltd, Elcograf S.p.A.

MIX
Paper | Supporting
responsible forestry
FSC® C104740
www.fsc.org FSC

Headline's policy is to use papers that are natural, renewable and recyclable
products and made from wood grown in well-managed forests and other
controlled sources. The logging and manufacturing processes are expected
to conform to the environmental regulations of the country of origin.

Headline Publishing Group Limited
An Hachette UK Company
Carmelite House
50 Victoria Embankment
London EC4Y 0DZ

The authorised representative in the EEA is Hachette Ireland,
8 Castlecourt Centre, Dublin 15, D15 XTP3, Ireland (email: info@hbgi.ie)

www.headline.co.uk
www.hachette.co.uk

# CONTENTS

## Act III: MONEY AND DRUGS, 1995–2012

## Act IV: GANG WARS, 2012–20

**EPILOGUE: 2020–Present Day**

## DEFINITION OF A MOB BOSS

A professional criminal who commands a gang of crooks involved in what the law likes to call a 'joint enterprise', to make money by any means available – protection rackets, extortion, loan sharking, smuggling, drug running, theft, burglary, handling stolen goods, armed robbery and money laundering. Often violence is involved.

# REALITY BITES

The mob is closer than you think. If you buy a £10 bag of weed to make a festival go with a swing or snort a line of coke after a middle-class dinner party, some money somewhere along the line is going to organised crime. The local dealer you buy your recreational drugs off may seem harmless enough, but they are the last in the link of a chain that leads from the person who grew the stuff to your front door. And that chain is run by the mob.

If you live in the inner city, gangsters will probably have a hand in any club or casino you visit. Restaurants, pubs, even local corner shops will, more than likely, be paying protection money. You will be paying part of that protection money on your bill.

And if you've walked down the silent streets at night and wondered how you stayed safe without seeing a single cozzer, that's also us. It's in the interests of people like me to keep petty crime away from our manor as much as we can. That way the Old Bill stay in their cosy cop shops, drinking cocoa, filling out their expenses and not bothering us.

So you shouldn't resent the ways you pay little bits of money to the mob. We perform a valuable social function. Sure, there's violence. But by and large, it's just between ourselves. Yes, there's armed robbery, but the last thing a blagger wants to do is hurt a civilian. Not just because it gets you serious jail time, but because we aren't here to hurt innocent people. We just want the money. If a villain takes out another bad guy, why should you care? There's one less criminal to bother about. It frees up cells in prison for other offenders.

It's a hard reality, but for you, the reader, arguably a better one for us being there.

# AUTHOR'S NOTE –
# NOTHING BUT THE TRUTH

This book contains details of numerous crimes. But I am not a grass. Many of the people involved in my story are dead or banged up. Nevertheless, I feel obliged to protect their identities. For the sake of their families and loved ones, I will use false names where appropriate. And while the particulars of their misdeeds may have been given a full airing in an open courtroom, I will change certain details to prevent their identification.

As for my own wrongdoing, I am currently out of the country in Northern Cyprus, which has no extradition treaty with the UK. Indeed, since the Turkish invasion in 1974, the Turkish Republic of Northern Cyprus has not even been recognised by any nation apart from Turkey. As far as the United Nations and the European Union are concerned, it does not exist, and so I am beyond the reach of the law. But things can change and there is no way that I am going to put down on the page anything that could be presented as evidence against me in a court of law, or might possibly implicate others.

Remember that I am not just in danger from the authorities. The British police may hold no sway here and the UK legal system has no influence, but real gangsters recognise no such jurisdiction. If anyone I have had dealings with feared any indiscretion on my part, it would be easy enough for them to pay a local gangster to bump me off. As a result, I think you will understand that I have to keep the facts of my own life somewhat hazy. Dates, places and descriptions have been altered to protect the guilty.

However, I have promised the publishers of this book that I will write as full and frank an account of my life in crime as is possible within those constraints. And as I have recently been diagnosed with terminal cancer, I have no reason not to tell you the truth, the whole truth and nothing but the truth, so help me God.

I also ought to issue the obligatory warning that some of the language in this book reflects the attitudes of the time, particularly where it comes to gender and race. And there are some descriptions of violence that some people may find distressing.

Hope you can stomach it.

ANONYMOUS

Girne, Turkish Republic of Northern Cyprus

October 2024

# INTRODUCTION

*I am a mob boss.* I know what that makes you think about . . .
either Al Capone in the 1920s spraying slugs around with a
Chicago piano or Marlon Brando with cotton wool in his
cheeks in *The Godfather*. But in many ways, it's not really like
that. Though in some it is. In the world of crime, you need to
trust your associates and it's easier if they are family. Think of
the Kray twins, the Richardsons, the Adams family . . .

The problem with these old geezers is that you know
about them. They made the papers. Most of us blokes involved
in organised crime treasure our anonymity. The law likes to
nick big names. They can't big themselves up for nicking
someone nobody knows. So you will never have heard of our
lot. We've gone to a lot of trouble to stay under the radar, so
I'm not even going to tell you our name. Just think of us – like
the Royal Family – as The Firm. That's right, going as generic
as we can.

You ought to know from the outset that I never wanted to
become a gangster, but I was born into a criminal family. My
dad and his brother were big-time blaggers. Consequently, my

dad was not around for much of my childhood, though I would see him every month or so in Wormwood Scrubs. I learned very early on that I did not want to spend time in there. After a bit of the usual petty thievery and fights as a teenager on the streets, I was determined to go straight. The rest is happenstance.

The problem was I didn't do very well in school. Our family generally did not get on well with authority. When the school wouldn't let me do what I wanted, I left prematurely. It was a mistake. I see that now. But, later, I got myself off to the Working Men's College in Camden. I'd always loved reading, devouring books by the dozen. That was an education in itself. Hence, I can write this without the aid of a ghostwriter.

From my deprived childhood in what were then the dark, grimy streets of North Kensington, I also realised the importance of money, so I went on to study accountancy. This would be the making of me.

I had two older brothers who followed Dad into the family profession – first in smash and grab, then armed robbery, protection and inevitably drugs. Along the way, they built up a handy team of useful people around them who would help in the family business. They soon had a problem with all the money they were making and, although I aimed to get married and lead a respectable life, I was brought back into the business to launder all that cash. Accountants can be useful, it turns out.

It was also good for the lads to have a business brain on the team. There were the clubs we took over to run, as well as launderettes, betting shops and casinos, all of which were easy places to launder cash. And there were bankers to deal with, whom my brothers would inevitably piss off.

Then when drugs came on the scene, they needed someone with a good business head on his shoulders to deal with the big wheels in Amsterdam and Latin America. These were multimillion-dollar deals which had to be done on the QT as far as the authorities were concerned.

Whether I wanted it or not, I became central to the functioning of The Firm. Just another gangster in a sharp suit. Only I didn't have to do any of the heavy work. My big brothers and their mates handled that. They were not averse to having a drink with The Filth either, if they thought those coppers could help grease the wheels of their operation.

Despite these connections, though, eventually one of my brothers got banged up. The other was killed by a gangland rival. Someone had to take care of business. That's how I reluctantly found myself as the boss. Then the wars between rival gangs heated up, and I had to turn hard man myself, and did some things I'm not happy about. That's why I had to leave the country and why I needed to get this story off my chest.

I hope it will act as a warning. One against a life of crime, against the ways of violence and against the path I have taken. Because as much as I had to do what I had to do, I'm not proud of it. So I hope you take a lesson or two from my tale.

# PROLOGUE – THE CRIMINAL UNDERWORLD

Sure, there's crime in the countryside. But it is in the cities that gangsters thrive, and the slums of post-war London were a breeding ground for criminals. The previous generation of gangsters modelled themselves on the mobsters of Chicago and New York they'd seen in the movies. But our heroes were closer to home. We looked up to the Krays and wanted to be like them. They were sharp and dapper – they even had their picture taken by celebrity fashion photographer David Bailey.

In our eyes, the Krays were up there with the Beatles and the Rolling Stones, and yet they were just like us, working class and from regular stock. They made it seem like the world was wide open to lads like me and my brothers. And although we were still playing on bomb sites, the rest of the country seemed to be swimming with money, so all we had to do was go out and take it. Kids like us deserved our share.

Having been let down by the educational system, what choice did most of us have? World War II was over before we were born. Conscription ended in 1960 so we would never have been forced to wear khaki, but National Service would at least have given us the opportunity to learn a trade and travel the world, even if it did mean getting shot at. Post-war austerity was coming to an end and the economy was picking up. Looking back, being a baby boomer should have been a lot of fun. It was, if you were middle class. But those at the bottom of the heap still looked forward to a life of drudgery, manual labour and poor wages. There was also the choice between slum housing, confinement in one of the shoddy tower blocks that were shooting up, or exile to a faceless council estate in a new town far away in the countryside. The only way out was music, acting, football, boozing, photography or crime. That's what we were dealing with. Not sure many of us felt we had an option.

# ACT I

## A LIFE OF CRIME

### 1956–82

# CHAPTER ONE
## MUM AND DAD

There used to be a photograph that stood, in a frame, on the mantelpiece in our flat when I was a kid. I wonder where it is now. It was in black and white and showed two people in a bleak urban landscape, blackened by coal smoke and damaged by bombs. Behind them is the Old Kensington Register Office. They were my mum and dad.

My father was in uniform with a single stripe on his sleeve. There were medal ribbons on his chest, though he didn't talk about what he had done in the war. I learned over the years that those who had actually fought on the front lines never talked about it. The loudmouths were always those at the rear echelons. They were full of war stories that did not ring true. Dad had little time for them. Nor did he have any time for Remembrance Sunday and the two minutes' silence. He wanted to forget, not remember.

My mother was wearing a knee-length cotton frock in a floral print with white peep-toe shoes. A small white hat was perched on top of her dark hair that was piled up on the top of her head in the elaborate fashion of the time. And she was carrying a huge bunch of rather bedraggled flowers.

She told me that she had done war work in a factory, though she had quit to become a housewife when the men came back from overseas. In the photograph, a sheepish smile played around her lips, maybe because she was happy, maybe because it was her wedding day, maybe something else. Dad looked stern and resigned. I guess the excitement of the war was over and there was little to look forward to in a London that had been bombed to rubble during the Blitz.

The post-war slump must have taken the edge off the raptures of young love. Whatever freedoms they had enjoyed during the disruption of the war itself had now fled. With the knot tied, their youth was well and truly over. It was time to settle down to the constraints of domestic life. At least that's the way it appeared in the photograph.

From what I remember, my parents were in love – though not in a showy way. People didn't back then. There was a genuine warmth between them and they seemed happy enough when they were together – which wasn't much given Dad's post-war career as a criminal.

Certainly, they were together enough to have two sons – I'll call them Steve and Mick – born in 1949 and 1951 respectively. Then it seems my father was away for a few years. I learned later that he and my uncle Jack had knocked over a post office. When Dad returned from prison, marital life resumed and I came along in 1956. By all accounts, it was a difficult birth. Mum and I almost died. She, it was discovered, had a weak heart, while I was born with the umbilical cord wrapped around my neck.

I was told that because I had had to fight for my life from my first moments in this world, it made me stronger, which I think is true. My mother, though, was advised to have no more kids. She had a hysterectomy which put paid to that.

In the fashion of the time, I was named after a film star. I won't tell you which one, but he was the lead in a gangster movie, appropriately enough. So throughout her life, I was, in my mother's eyes, a glamorous matinee idol. I hope I did not disappoint, even though I was a slow starter when it came to the ladies, though I was too young to think about it then.

We lived in a squalid block in North Kensington. I know Kensington sounds posh, but the fancy part was to the south, beyond Notting Hill Gate down to Fulham Road. We lived at the other end of Ladbroke Grove which is actually Kensal Town – or 'The Town' as we called it.

Although the buildings had been condemned in the 1930s, they were still inhabited. At least one family occupied each of the four floors. There was a communal entrance and the shared khazi was in a concrete yard that backed on to the railway lines that ran in and out of Paddington. The post-war building boom had yet to catch up with us.

The family had lived in a single room until I came along.

Then the housing trust gave us two rooms on a higher floor – one for eating in, one for sleeping in, we decided. As the economy picked up in the 1960s, our block was finally demolished and we were moved down the street into a place that had three rooms and a cooker on the landing outside. It was still cramped, but that did not matter too much to us kids as no one in the street owned a car. That meant that Steve and Mickey could play with the other kids on the road outside. And besides that, there were still bomb sites to explore. For me with my little legs, it was hard to keep up and I was more of a mummy's boy, I guess, so I spent more of the time at home.

I also went with Mum on the various charring jobs in the posh houses of Ladbroke Grove and South Kensington where she cleaned to make ends meet. When her employers were entertaining in the evenings, she would help with the catering. I would have to sit in the kitchen and behave. Anyway, that way I got to see how other people lived and I swore that one day I would live in a house like those where Mum cleaned – and that she would too.

Unfortunately, Dad was not a great provider. He earned money as a rent collector for a local slum landlord, but he spent most of it in the private drinking clubs and spielers that were springing up. This brought him into the company of the smart-suited young gangsters who were taking advantage of the 1960s boom.

Though Dad's boozing and gambling caused friction with Mum – and I think he was also a bit of a ladies' man – he was generous with his winnings, so they would soon make up. At least, he called the money he brought home his winnings, though I now suspect that they were the proceeds of some form of crime.

Steve and Mick looked up to Dad and he spoilt them rotten. They also admired his new-found friends, in the mohair suits and flashy cars. Then there was Uncle Jack who, despite not having any visible means of support, drove around in a white Jag. He too derived his income from crime. After the war, Dad and Uncle Jack seem to have decided that that was the way to indulge their taste for adventure. Or, perhaps, it really was the only way available to go in life back then.

Of course, I didn't think of us as a crime family. Dad's father had died long before I was born and I don't know much about him, but Nan lived nearby in an estate. We would go over there on Sunday morning. For us, her flat seemed to be the height of luxury, with an inside toilet and a bath, albeit in the kitchen. She even had a settee and carpet in what she called the living room. What's more, it didn't smell of damp!

We didn't used to stay long as Dad would go to the pub which opened at twelve. Steve and Mick would be left outside – kids weren't allowed in pubs back then – with a glass of squash. They would horse around while I went home with

Mum who would cook the Sunday dinner. The pubs chucked out at two in the afternoon on a Sunday and Dad would return well refreshed. Steve and Mick would have scrapes and bruises as their horsing around inevitably turned into a scrap. We had no TV back then, so we had to listen to the radio, or the wireless as we called it. Needless to say, we never went to church.

Mum had come from Cardiff. Her mum had died when she was young and her father was strict. She had won a scholarship to a Catholic school, but he refused to shell out for the uniform, so she could not take up her place. When she finished her cursory secondary education, she left home to live with friends and got a job at the Co-op, then sought out the bright lights of London where she met my dad. The premature curtailment of her education left her with a thirst for reading and she encouraged me in this. By the time I could walk, she signed me up at the library in Ladbroke Grove. Under her influence, I would read reasonably well by the time I went to school and that set me on the path to fulfil the task I am undertaking now. She also took out library tickets for Steve and Mick, but they didn't use them. You could take out five books on each ticket, so I took all fifteen.

After infant school, I joined my brothers at primary school. Already, they were getting into trouble with the teachers. They were the kings of the playground and anyone who challenged them could be sure of a fight. Small though I was, no one would dare to take my lunch money off me as they would have my big brothers to deal with. They extended their protection to my friend, Terry, which would set us in good stead in later life.

Sometimes, after school, I was allowed to go around to Terry's place. His family had two floors of a four-storey house just around the corner from Latimer Road Tube station. Not only did they have a light and airy front room where no one cooked or slept, but they also had a glass-fronted bookcase that contained the *Encyclopaedia Britannica*, a bunch of second-hand hardback classics – *Robinson Crusoe*, *Treasure Island*, *Tom Sawyer* – and the works of Charles Dickens. These meant little to Terry. He was a cricketer, a footballer and the star of our annual sports day. I always loved football, but he got me interested in cricket too.

While I had protection at school, the streets were still dangerous, not just for kids but for adults too. There were marauding gangs of teens and men would fight outside the pubs on a Saturday night. One day, I was going to school carrying my prized collection of cigarette cards when an older boy stopped me. He threatened to wallop me unless I showed them to him. When I did, he grabbed them and ran off. I did not cry, but I realised that I had to toughen up. Steve and Mick would not have let that happen to them.

The only way to survive in the mean streets of Kensal Town was to fight. Dad tried to teach me how to box, but I was always a disappointment. In frustration I would punch and punch and punch as hard as I could. But he was a big man and my infantile flailing made little impression. When my dad and I would fight, Mum had to step in when he got through my defences and landed a punch on my skinny body. Steve and Mick made a better fist of it and he soon signed them up with the boxing club in the Harrow Road.

Outside of our boxing matches, Dad never beat me – a common way of enforcing parental discipline back then. Teachers were also authorised to beat you. It was a thing I sought to avoid, though Steve and Mick took regular whacks. Kids were inspired by the regular fare of the Saturday morning cinema, as cowboy films always featured a barroom brawl and gangster movies had the obligatory shoot-out.

There were some adventures though. Terry and I took some wheels from an abandoned pram, a fruit crate and some other bits of wood to make a box cart. In it, we'd speed down the hill to Ladbroke Grove Tube station. Later we'd scavenge for bits of old bikes and build our own. Then we would race around the streets pretending we were on motorbikes.

One day, when I was haring round a corner, I crashed into a pedestrian who had just come out of a corner store, knocking his groceries all over the street.

'You little f***ing idiot,' he yelled, waving his fist at me. 'Why don't you learn to f***ing ride a bike?'

But I was not going to be intimidated. I had a means of escape and I sped off down the road, leaving him far behind. I was not as well equipped as my big brothers to deal with the world, but with my trusty bike I could at least get out of scrapes.

I learned another lesson on the streets of North Kensington. One afternoon, I was walking home from school with Terry and Curtis, a Black kid I had met in my infant school, when some deranged youth grabbed me and held a broken bottle to my face, inches from my eye. The streets were full of broken glass in those days. I guess the guy was mentally ill. Terry and Curtis could have run off and left me, but they stayed with me while this nutcase dragged me around the streets for an hour or so.

None of the adults we passed tried to do anything about it. But I wasn't on my own. My mates stayed with me. Finally, the nutter was distracted by something – a motorbike backfiring, I think it was – and I wriggled free. We ran down the road to a street with big houses on where we dived through a hedge. The houses there had huge front gardens which we had explored before, much to the annoyance of the residents. Once through the front hedge we could make our way from garden to garden without appearing back on the pavement.

Eventually, when we emerged back on to the street, there was no sign of the nutjob. I had learned to hold my nerve in the face of danger and the value of having friends you can depend on in adversity. Loyalty is everything.

Curtis wasn't the only Black boy in school, but they were few and far between back then. Mainly, the people who looked like Curtis were young men who had come over from the Caribbean seeking to establish themselves in the UK. Their wives and children came later. Mum got on with them while Dad harboured many of the prejudices of his generation. Not that he was worried about them coming over here to take our jobs as so many did back then. He was no great fan of working. Besides, he found it best to swallow any bigotry when he was collecting their rent. It was easier if you were friendly, especially when large numbers of them were crammed into a single house by the slum landlord he worked for. He could, of course, be menacing if he thought they were taking the piss.

I was too young to remember the riots and stabbings of the 1950s, but there were still Teddy boys on the streets and there was always an uneasy atmosphere of menace about. But at primary school we all got on and Curtis was a bright and popular kid. Looking back, though, I'm sure that he must have suffered racial taunts and harassment outside school. Few people cared to mind their racist language back then.

It meant little to Terry and me as Curtis was a great footballer. We would play in the park together and Dad would sometimes take us to Loftus Road to see Queens Park Rangers. He wasn't so good at cricket (none of us were), but then it is harder to play cricket with just three of you anyway. Lord's was not far away, but that was not for the likes of us. Looking back, I wish. . .

Steve and Mick didn't come to Loftus Road with us. They went with the crew, the Bushbabies, hoping for a fight. I don't know how they got the money – from thieving, I guess – but they used to go to away games too which is how they chummed up with like-minded football hooligans around the country. People who loved nothing more than a beer and a fight on a Saturday afternoon. Later they got together with England supporters. This gave them the chance to travel abroad, coming back with all sorts of designer gear which they sold at school. The stuff was clearly nicked as they sometimes were away from home longer than they anticipated, spending a little time in foreign jails where they said they met up with local criminals. At first, I never believed them, but then I started to see signs of a pretty decent network of underworld contacts around the country and across the Continent.

To get away from our rough old streets, Terry, Curtis and I would cycle up to Kensington Gardens to play there, or go to Holland Park with its peacocks and adventure playground.

And if we wanted to go further, we'd head for the barren wasteland of Wormwood Scrubs, which was overlooked by the gloomy walls of the famous prison. A bunch of us went out to investigate an old army camp there one night. There were turrets and concrete bunkers overgrown with grass and weeds.

Pretending to be soldiers, we played war games. One day, Terry, with his tenuous grasp of history, told us the unlikely story that the camp had been run by the Japanese and they had baked British soldiers in ovens there. It was the sort of thing you might just about believe when you were ten. Anyway, he insisted that we investigate.

A slope ran down to what must have been underground living quarters, though the roof had long since collapsed. Terry took the lamp from his bike and led the way. In a wall there were three large openings, which looked like they could have been ovens. I froze, but Curtis poked around inside, looking for a shard of bone or a tooth that might have survived the flames. Convinced that we were about to make some vital discovery, Terry swore us all to secrecy. We found nothing, of course.

We returned to the 'death camp' several times during the week to continue our search, but found nothing more sinister than an empty tin of Spam. The place was always deserted and the only people who might have been aware of our investigations were solitary dog walkers and lost souls peering out of the tiny barred windows of Her Majesty's Prison Wormwood Scrubs.

With the Swinging Sixties now in full flow, life began to get better. Our block was due to be demolished and the housing trust moved us to four rooms occupying the bottom two floors of a terraced house. We had a kitchen cum living room. Mum and Dad had their own bedroom. Steve and Mick shared, and I had a small box room to myself. Mum persuaded the trust to install a makeshift bathroom in the basement. The toilet was still in the backyard, though.

By then, Steve and Mick had moved on to secondary school and I was getting ready to sit my eleven-plus. One day, Dad and Uncle Jack came home with a record player and some Beatles records. We also got a TV, just in time to watch England win the World Cup. The whole atmosphere in the country had changed. We were fired with optimism. I soon passed my eleven-plus and was on my way to my own grammar school. Dad was so flushed with money at that time that he didn't grumble about buying the uniform.

When the police came round, it was clear where the money for the record player and TV had come from. Dad and Uncle Jack had been on a burgling spree. They got eight years each. It was a heavy sentence because they already had long records from before I was born.

Of course, in our neighbourhood, we had little time for the police. We hardly ever saw them on the streets. They did not walk the beat or quell the occasional outbreak of racial violence that had plagued the area. In fact, when they did intervene, it seemed to make things worse. The Caribbeans I talked to thought they were racist – not without good reason – and the whites had more time for the criminals. They were more like us. Looking back, I guess, in the spirit of the sixties, we were all anti-Establishment.

In our family, we took our cue from our dad, who was old school. The cops were the enemy. If there was any problem, we could sort it out between ourselves. We didn't need the rozzers to do it for us. There was honour among thieves. We were just trying to get by and you never grassed up your mates.

# CHAPTER TWO
## STEVE AND MICK

Steve and Mick followed Dad's criminal code from the start. The big kids in the playground, they took no stick from anyone. Steve was a natural leader. What he said went. If you didn't like it, there was Mick to deal with. He was handy with his fists. They both were, but Mick had a look in his eye that told you not to go there unless you wanted the beating of your life.

Their criminal life had started with stealing sweets. Remember rationing had only just come to an end and there was still a shortage. We'd had no money anyway, so if you got a couple of kids together in a newsagents, it was easy enough for one to get the old bloke behind the counter distracted while the others grabbed what they could and we all made a run for it.

It didn't even have to be that blatant. In those days, sweets were sold loose, so you could pocket as many as you wanted while the old geezer was looking the other way. He wouldn't know what was missing until later – if at all. Now, with my accountant's hat on, I would put this down to ineffective stocktaking.

When Mum was short of cash, we'd pull the same stunts on grocers just to put food on the table. We weren't the only ones in the area who had to turn to shoplifting to survive. It was the way it had to be.

Once Dad was banged up and the stolen bunce he'd left us was gone, there was still the rent and lecky to pay. Money was required. So Steve and Mick turned the local propensity to shoplift into a nice little protection racket. For five bob a week, they told the shopkeepers that they would stop other kids nicking from them, which was not hard as it was them that was doing most of the nicking in the first place.

They also went dipping. The bus stops at Notting Hill Gate and along Kensington High Street promised rich pickings for pickpockets with small hands, deft fingers and fast legs to run away with a wallet, purse or handbag. And everyone carried cash back then, so you could just lift the money and dump the purse or wallet. Mum did not ask where the money came from.

Even before they left school, Steve and Mick were big lads. I could contribute little to the household funds, except when they started housebreaking because I was small enough to squeeze through half-opened windows or skylights. Otherwise, as a puny runt in a grammar school uniform, I could hardly be intimidating. But I could be intimidated.

In our area, all the tough kids were going to the secondary

modern. Terry and Curtis had also passed the eleven-plus and were going to the grammar school with me. In our posh school uniforms, we were bound to be picked on. Curtis's colour didn't help, but he was my mate.

On the way home from school, Curtis and I had to walk along the fringe of the White City Estate, which a gang of local yobs claimed as their territory. There were going to be problems. The clue was in the name. It was a very white area and the kids there were made for trouble. When they saw us, there was bound to be a confrontation. First, they wanted to pick on Curtis just because he was Black. When I stuck up for him, I was called a 'wog lover'. That was enough for me to get beaten up constantly.

I'd return home bruised and bleeding, and would try and keep it to myself. But when Steve and Mick saw this, they wanted to know what had happened. I told them and they were not having it. The next day, they went down there with us and called the White City Mob out. There were a handful of them led by a big geezer named, I think, Dave. Though Steve, who was only sixteen, was a lot smaller than this guy, he walked right up to him and smashed him in the face. We were outnumbered, of course, but that did not seem to matter to Mick who pitched in with such ferocity it scared me. When it was all over and Dave was bleeding profusely and the rest of them were on the floor or had run away, Mick was still punching and kicking the bodies on the street until Steve had to stop him. It was carnage.

Steve and Mick were used to this sort of thing from their time at football games. But it was the first time that I had been involved in any kind of group violence. It was something I had wanted to stay away from, but I guess with my background it was something I couldn't escape for long. My family were a gang in their own right.

While this was the start of an enduring feud with the WCM, there were immediate benefits. It gave us a reputation in the area, even with the bullies at school. The worst of them was a guy called Voytek, whose gang of Polish boys from Acton terrorised the younger boys. The idea that they might get a visit from my two big brothers meant that they left me, Terry and Curtis alone – though when it came to Curtis, there was the usual name-calling.

As I said, Steve and Mick looked up to Dad. He was a blagger. Though he did not bring much of the money he made through criminal activities back to Mum, they admired his lifestyle. He and Uncle Jack had hung out in a club where most of the white criminals used to gather, along with a bunch of local prostitutes. Uniformed 'cuntstables', as the patrons pointedly called them, used to raid regularly to pick up the girls for 'living off immoral earnings', particularly after a machine selling rubber johnnies was installed in the ladies.

In 1962, a Jamaican took over the gaff, but things went on much the same, except that weed was now on the menu. Black and white mixed and were united in one thing. Neither wanted anything to do with the police, though some plain-clothed cops would still come in for a free drink sometimes just to make the point that no one was beyond the law. Cops and crims were not so different when you think about it. They could reach an accommodation, which might prove useful later. Dad had had no time for them though. 'Coppers are like Germans,' he said. 'The only good one's a dead one.' I guess he was speaking for his generation.

Dad used the club until he was banged up and would take Steve and Mick along. As a club you were, I think, legally allowed to take children in, even though they were banned from pubs – not that anyone would have taken any notice of the rules away. My brothers loved the company of the old geezers (particularly the really shifty ones) that Dad used to rub shoulders with. They were role models.

Later, my brothers would visit when they had stolen goods they wanted to unload. Usually there was someone who would take dodgy gear off them for a few bob. Even the old lags still had contacts. By that time, the stuff still came from burgling but thankfully, I had soon grown big enough not to be dragooned into helping them. I couldn't fit through small gaps any more.

Steve and Mick also made money 'rolling' prostitutes' clients. They would persuade the girl to take her John to an isolated spot where they could catch him defenceless, in the act, and rob him. If he had a car, they would yank open the doors and rifle through his belongings. Prostitutes were not keen on this as it lost them valuable customers, but the threats and inducements they were offered left them no choice.

Otherwise, Steve and Mick made their money by extending their protection racket to small-time bookmakers, some of whom continued to trade after off-track betting was legalised in 1960. There were other gambling dens and spielers that would pay up, if appropriate pressure was applied.

Things did not always go smoothly between my brothers. I never knew what the fights were about. Both were boxers and, while Steve was older and bigger, Mick sometimes got the better of him. I wanted nothing to do with these scraps. Besides, both were fiercely protective of me. And despite their fights, they were always there to back one another up if someone turned on them.

There used to be a bank holiday funfair on Wormwood Scrubs common with boxing booths offering £5 to anyone who could go the distance with a professional. When Steve stepped forward to take up the challenge, the crowds laughed. He looked too young and skinny to take on a heavyweight, so the gaffer asked for a volunteer from the crowd. Finding no other taker, Mick stepped forward. Soon they were stripped to the waist in the makeshift ring and the crowd were cheering.

They were well matched, each giving as good as they got. Steve ended up with a bloody nose, while Mick had the makings of two black eyes. Eventually the fight was declared a draw and the barker gave them ten bob each.

Dad had started entering them in local competitions. Both of them could have had a career in fighting, but once Dad went to jail, they found themselves too occupied with their other job.

After the war, when Dad had been in his heyday, the police largely left the area alone. But following the race riots in 1958 and the murder of Kelso Cochrane, they felt that they had to take more of an interest. They got wind of Steve and Mick's protection racket when a local shopkeeper failed to make his weekly payment and found his shop being trashed. Steve and Mick were already well known to the Old Bill and could expect no mercy from the juvenile courts. They were convicted of criminal damage and sent to one of the remaining borstals at Banstead in Surrey.

Already, Mum was taking me to visit Dad in prison – first in Pentonville, then in Wormwood Scrubs. These places were grim. Although the Clean Air Act had been passed soon after I was born – introducing smokeless fuel to banish London's famous 'peasouper' fogs – these old Victorian buildings were still caked with grime from coal fires. If that did not make them look grim enough, they were worse inside.

Of course, we did not see the cramped cells, often shared, with a bucket for a toilet that had to be 'slopped out' every morning. But you could smell the stench. There was the dreadful clank of the doors, the loud click of the heavy locks being opened and closed, the sharp jangle of the keys, the bag and pocket search, and the quick pat-down.

Then you were in the visiting room where the prison officers kept an eye on every move. They was no touching and no cakes with files in them being handed over. The strip lighting drained everything of colour. Everything seemed grey even when Mum wore her most colourful hat.

Steve and Mick did not seem to have minded this at all. There was always something going on between them. Dad loved seeing them. But when they were banged up too and it was just Mum and me visiting, we found little to talk to Dad about. It was like going to see an elderly relative on their deathbed. I could not wait for visiting hours to be over. As Dad's sentence dragged on, I made excuses not to go. The one thing it taught me was that I never wanted to end up in prison.

Visiting Steve and Mick in Banstead Hall in Surrey with Mum was far nicer. It looked like a country house set in spacious grounds, though the regime for the boys was tough. The brothers also told me that there were some tough characters in there, but they could handle themselves. They had backup – each other. The worst part of visiting was that it took more than an hour on the train, then it was a long walk from the station.

My brothers were city boys and loved being out on the streets. They hated being cooped up in the dormitories, and fresh air and the countryside did not exactly thrill them either. However, they flourished when surrounded by others who had chosen the same path. They thrived with the rivalry. It soon became clear to me that they had quickly developed the ambition to be the best of the worst – or the worst of the worst, whichever way you want to think about it. However hard the environment, they were determined to be top dogs. What's more, they had plenty of time for boxing practice – both in the ring and in the fights that often broke out on the wing.

When they got out, they decided to turn professional and were looking forward to a promising career in the world of boxing. They worked their way up in competitive bouts and, one time, got to fight at the Albert Hall. Steve won his bout, but Mick was disqualified. Sometimes he was too aggressive and could not control himself. The money for these professional bouts was not much cop, but they supplemented their income with a bit more thievery.

Local businesses had been advised not to keep money on the premises overnight. That meant that someone would have to take cash to the local bank's night safe at the end of the business day. Usually some junior employee or someone approaching retirement age would be delegated to carry the takings down the street. This was stupid. Out on the street alone, they would be vulnerable, particularly as the winter evenings drew in.

Soon after the brothers came home from borstal, violence on the streets around our way increased. While they had been away, other gangs had tried to muscle in on their rackets. Steve and Mick decided that they had to be taught a lesson. An eighteen-year-old from one of the new council estates was found in bad shape in an alley off Portobello Road. The story was that he had been beaten with a bicycle chain. Despite his injuries, he kept his mouth firmly shut. Mick was already known for being handy with a knife and was not above slashing a grass across the face.

The story of the attack made the local paper. A girl had apparently witnessed the attack, but when there was a preliminary hearing at the magistrates' court, she mysteriously suffered from amnesia. The victim was no more forthcoming. The police made enquiries but, getting nowhere, they dropped the matter.

Some weeks later, Steve got into trouble again when he got into a fight with a young copper who had given him some lip in Notting Hill Gate. It was the middle of the day and it's a busy street, so there were plenty of witnesses. He ended up in the cells. Meanwhile, Mick tracked down the copper and gave him a smack as well. Both of them got beaten up in the police station, deepening their hatred of The Filth. In court, they were lucky to escape with six months in the nick, a fine of £10 and probation. They were not too unhappy about it, and being sent to Wormwood Scrubs meant they could spend some time with Dad.

On their way to prison, the cozzers told them that if they had any more trouble from them, they'd smash their faces in. The brothers begged them to try. They weren't afraid of anything and knew that the only way ahead for them was crime. Their conviction put paid to their boxing careers. In the UK at least, promoters like to keep their sport appearing clean and don't like boxers who are known convicts. But prison presented other opportunities. After getting their basic criminal schooling in borstal, the nick became their university of crime. There were all sorts in there – thieves, thugs, shoplifters, burglars, blaggers and heavies, each with their individual skills which they were willing to share. It was the best education you could get if you wanted to be a serious mobster.

# CHAPTER THREE
## CAREER CRIMINALS

When Steve and Mick came out of the Scrubs, they had few prospects. With a criminal record and minimal education, they were unlikely to find a decent job, even if they had wanted one.

With no way to make a living, they took to other things full-time, starting with what came to be known as ram raiding. They would smash a stolen car through the window of a jeweller's shop and grab what they could. The proceeds would then be fenced through contacts they had made at Dad's old club.

Where they learned to drive I don't know (neither of them had ever had any lessons), but some of their mates in borstal were in for nicking cars and bikes. There were others in the area that had those skills.

The problem with ram raiding was that, having usually written off the car on impact, they had no easy means of escape, so they had to leg it through the streets with their hands full of ruby rings and diamond bracelets while alarm bells sounded. So they changed to nicking motorbikes instead and then they'd just chuck a brick through the jeweller's window, grab the loot and speed off.

Now flush, my big brothers were out a lot – dancing, picking up girls and fighting. There were always plenty of fights in dance halls, sometimes spilling out on to the street outside. The violence scared off some of the girls, meaning fewer guys would turn up, cutting the takings. So these venues began hiring doormen to quell the aggro. Mick took on a couple of these security gigs, largely for the bovver, as he didn't need the money. Steve was too fly for this type of work. He wouldn't want to risk blood splattering on to one of his flashy new suits.

Also, with their boxing careers long gone, there was no need for long runs around the streets at six o'clock in the morning or going to bed early at night. Instead, they lived in the night. They'd lounge around indoors all day, occasionally catnapping, and then stay out till the early hours. Mum and I knew it was best not to ask where they'd been or what they had been doing. We really didn't want to know.

And now that they did have money, the brothers decided that Mum had lived in squalor long enough and needed a new home. But she didn't want to move out to the countryside away from all her friends. With Dad still inside, she wanted to keep her family around her and the brothers needed to stay in the area to take care of business.

Home ownership was not something our family was familiar with. It was something the posh people at the other end of Ladbroke Grove did and, without regular, on-the-books employment, the brothers were in no position to get a mortgage. The purchase had to be in cash.

At the time, the slums of Notting Hill were getting a makeover. Immigration restrictions meant that not so many West Indians were coming over from the Caribbean. Those that had been here earlier had established themselves and moved to find better housing, often over the river in Brixton or the new estates in North London. There had been a crackdown on slum landlords and Notting Hill was showing the beginnings of gentrification.

With eleven grand in cash, they were able to purchase a three-storey house in the area. It even had a back garden. A local lawyer, who did not ask too many questions about where the money had come from, handled the paperwork. Of course, it was not in a great state of repair, but there were plenty of handymen in the area willing to do a bit of making good for extra cash. The boys had a reputation in the neighbourhood so it was understood that the Inland Revenue would not need to know.

Mum, for the first time, experienced the new-found luxury of deciding on the decoration of her own home, instead of living with what the housing trust had provided. By the time we moved in, the place was a palace. Mum had quit her job charring and now spent her time planting stuff in the garden, which became her pride and joy.

When Dad got out of prison, we had a welcome-home barbecue in the garden with all his old mates. With little to occupy his time, he took over the heavy gardening work from Mum, digging and weeding. Later, he found an added incentive when he dug up a couple of bin bags full of cash that the brothers had buried. The problem they had was they could not easily pay their ill-gotten gains into a bank or building society. Someone might ask where all this cash had come from.

At the time, I was also not doing well at school. English was the only thing I enjoyed. When was history, geography or maths ever going to come in useful in my life? History was over. Geography? When was I going to go anywhere? And maths? As long as I could count money and add up, what was the good of algebra or geometry? As for biology, I'd already learned as much as I needed to know from older boys. The conversation at school was largely confined to sex and football. So my schooldays were largely a matter of skiving off and spending time at home reading.

Crime was big in the newspapers of the time. There'd been the Great Train Robbery. Every local criminal wanted to pull off a blag like that and walk away with millions – except, of course, the Great Train Robbers hadn't walked away. Most of them got banged up. Those who escaped were soon skint, while someone else had scarpered with most of the cash.

After the Great Train Robbers, the next role models were the Kray twins. All the local criminals wanted to be like them. They were celebrities. Steve and Mick adopted their style and ventured up West for their clubbing. While most of their generation got their gear from chic boutiques on the King's Road in Chelsea and Carnaby Street, Steve and Mick were strictly Savile Row, like Ronnie and Reggie.

My brothers also began hanging out in pubs and clubs where the proper bad guys were. The boys would not take any disrespect from the old-timers, as dis would be met with a slap. And when I say 'slap', I mean with a fist. More than one jaw was broken.

Among ordinary punters, they commanded respect. The sixties was the era of counter-culture. Everyone was anti the Establishment, and Steve and Mick definitely did not embrace the straight life. They were seen as outsiders who lived life on their own terms. It was the spirit of the times. How they could afford to live their lifestyle without going to work, no one asked. Again, no one wanted to know.

But when the Krays were sent down in 1969, everything changed. They had got away with it for so long, but now it appeared that they were not invincible. They got life imprisonment with a minimum of thirty years, but it was clear to everyone that they were never coming out.

That was the moment Steve and Mick quickly realised

that it wasn't a good idea to cultivate a high profile. They returned to Notting Hill and The Town, and hid in the shadows. That did not mean they were going to give up crime. They would just go about it more discreetly and stay out of the limelight as much as they could.

In The Town there was an old cinema called the Regal. When the chain started closing down, it had been converted into a snooker hall. Local gangs hung out there. It was hardly a going venture as they put the screws on the manager and there was a rumour that he was going to shut up shop.

Steve and Mick paid a visit. Steve was a bit of a sportsman and liked to play, while Mick was always more keen on watching who was coming in and out. It was plain the place was on its last legs. There were a number of fights on the premises. Snooker halls are particularly vulnerable because the green baize on the tables rips easily. Rubbish piled in the alley round the back caught fire. Fed up with the hassle, the manager quit. The owners were keen to sell up and my brothers took over.

As soon as they were in charge, the fighting stopped. The tables were re-covered. The place was redecorated and the bar restocked. Open twenty-four hours a day, the place was soon back in profit. It was a magnet for whoever the brothers had met in borstal and prison, and the locals who did business with them. Some of Dad's old mates would drop by in the hope of getting a free drink. They were full of stories of the good old days. Dad had been a legend back then, until he went to jail, of course.

Then there was a new influx of people who wanted to make deals with Mick and Steve. It was a pool of illegal activity and the centre of their operations. That, of course, attracted other gangsters who thought they could move in on the action.

The White City Mob paid a visit. They had tied up with an Italian group calling themselves the Shepherd's Bush Mafia. They did not live up to their name and were quickly dispatched after Mick clumped one punter with a snooker cue and knocked another out with the cue ball. Nevertheless, the brothers took the threat that was put to them seriously. After that, they got tooled up.

The guns they'd bought were not on show in case the Old Bill dropped by, but people knew they were there. That, they figured, was enough of a deterrent. Or at least, that was Steve's reasoning. Mick was always itching to play around with them. It seemed to him that, in the world back then, these were the tools of the trade. He was right. Pretty soon, the inner circle in the snooker hall would form themselves into a gang with Steve the boss and Mick as enforcer.

Steve had the brains and everyone knew you could reason with him. Once you had lost the argument, you had Mick to deal with. He could never be persuaded to back down and never hesitated to use violence. His reputation as a nutcase made people make a deal with Steve in case Mick was unleashed. That was not going to be good for your health.

While they were succeeding in business, I was still failing at school, getting a grade A O level only in English, but failing in the other arts subjects. In the sciences, I got a B in physics, which I found relatively self-evident until relativity came along. After all, laws of mass and conservation of energy are really double-entry bookkeeping. But I only got a C in maths. My algebra and geometry let me down. I never understood chemistry. And biology? It was all about plants and animals. I was a city boy.

In the sixth form, I wanted to do English, physics and maths, but the headmaster said I had to choose between the humanities and the sciences. Much as I loved English, where would it lead? Being a writer was out of the question. I didn't want to be an English teacher and I couldn't really see any other use for it. So I was persuaded to sign up for physics, maths and higher maths. This was a mistake. Though I was good at arithmetic, I was soon out of my depth with trigonometry and calculus. Without the necessary mathematical skills, physics was soon beyond my grasp, so I simply dropped out. What point was there in continuing? Was I going to go to university with the posh kids? I didn't think so.

Perhaps I should have stuck with it back then. But people

like me did not become writers. Besides, I had nothing to write about. I knew nothing about the world. Who wants to read about a downbeat childhood in the back streets of Kensal Town?

Not that I was one of those people who was eager to leave school so they could go out to work. There was no great work ethic in our family, at least not on the male side. Mum had always grafted to put food on the table. But Dad and Uncle Jack, when they got out of prison, never got proper jobs. And Steve and Mick had no ambitions in the world of work.

Mum and Dad soon got tired of me hanging around the house all day, so I would go out for long walks around the area that would often end up at the Regal where I would bum a drink off someone. Usually my brothers' mates would help out, perhaps hoping to ingratiate themselves with Mick and Steve. I knew that they were gangsters and the money they spent was not honestly come by, but that did not matter. I had never been one particularly troubled by morals. What put me off crime was going to jail.

But Steve didn't like me bumming off his friends. He didn't like owing any favours to anyone and thought that I should feel the same. We were family and should put up a united front. Mick was eager to help out with a little cash, so he gave me some on the QT, but Steve didn't like this either. If I was on the payroll, then he thought I should join The

Firm. They knew that I didn't want to join them blagging, strong-arming and the other things they got up to. Besides, they had decided that their little brother definitely did not have the bottle.

Mick solved the problem by giving me a bar job. He justified this to Steve by telling him that it was better to have someone behind the bar they could trust. Barmen overhear things and they could be sure my lips were sealed. I wasn't going to go and grass them up.

Working behind the bar, I really began to see what was going on. It was from that vantage point, I guess, I learned the trade. Steve took care of business from a back room – an old storeroom converted into an office. Mick liked a more public arena. He had his own comfortable high-backed drawing-room chair in the snooker room. No one else dared sit there, even when he wasn't around. If someone new sat in Mick's chair by mistake, they would be told to move in no uncertain terms. And if Mick was about, they risked his wrath.

Mick liked the atmosphere of the snooker room with its low lights over the tables and the way it showed the thick fog of tobacco smoke. You could smoke indoors back then. He liked the fug and encouraged it by handing out cigarettes. For Mick, it was a movie set, like a scene from one of those old black-and-white classics. He loved classic gangster movies and he played the part in his V-lapelled double-breasted suits and with the gold rings on his fingers that doubled as a knuckle-duster. He sat in his chair facing the door, checking on who was coming in and basically holding court. Those wanting to speak to him would be invited to sit on a low stool beside him so that he could look down on them.

He brought in guests of his own. They were a bizarre selection. He liked freaks – giants, roly-polies, dwarves and midgets. One time he brought in a chimpanzee which he pretended to teach to talk. That did not last long after it began to shit all over the place. The other problem was that it did not get on with his savage Rottweiler – the tough guy's dog of choice until the pit bull and XL bully came along. He would beat it with a riding crop he found to stop it becoming soft and boast that no one else could handle it.

Old mates of my brothers began to confide in me because Steve had grown distant, locked in his little cupboard, while Mick had become more menacing. People were afraid to approach Mick in case they set him off. So mine became the ears of choice if they wanted to get a message to the family.

Fortunately, Mick usually preferred to take his aggression out on other mobs whom he viewed as the enemy. He would lead what were essentially raiding parties on the various boozers that local gangs used as their headquarters. Either the other gang would shrink away or the result would be an almighty bundle – involving knives, coshes and broken bottles and glasses. Mick would consider intimidating the enemy a victory, but he also loved a fight, so it was a win–win for him.

These outings always headed west – Shepherd's Bush, White City, Acton – or north – Kilburn, Harlesden, Willesden, Cricklewood, Wembley. Steve had decided that we should stay out of the West End for the moment to maintain our low profile.

Thankfully, I was spared these trips. I had to stay behind in the snooker hall to hold the fort, but I heard all the gruesome details when they got back. And they were gruesome. While some of the crew held back, Mick always pitched in full force. Steve liked to join in too. He enjoyed a scrap as well. But it was Mick that would go the distance, cutting up his opponent and putting the boot in. A fan of the film *A Clockwork Orange* (he had a pirated video of it after it was banned), he called this 'ultraviolence'. Apparently, this look of pure hatred came over his face – much like the guy in the movie, I imagine.

The key to their fighting style was hit first and hit hard. There was to be no faffing about. It was all or nothing. And they did their homework. The brothers would seek out information on rival gangs. They were to find out who the hard men were, who had to be taken out first. If they had a reputation for knife fights, Mick would carry a razor-sharp cutlass.

If they were tooled up, Mick too would carry a shooter and make sure the opposition knew it. It also circulated that he took the time to file the tips of the slugs, turning them into dumdum bullets that would blast holes in their victims.

Mick always knew how to start a fight. If there was an initial stand-off, he would come over all friendly. He would offer the opposition's top man a cigarette. When he opened his mouth to put it in, Mick would give him a devastatingly quick left hook. An open jaw breaks easily, as many found out to their cost. He would practise this for hours in front of the mirror and with a punchbag. The key he found was to engage the victim eyeball to eyeball. Then he would never see that smack coming from the side. With the sucker sprawled on the floor begging for someone to call an ambulance, the rest of the opposition would usually melt away.

Not only did these outings give the brothers a fearsome reputation throughout West and North London, it also kept their own troops in order. Having seen Mick and Steve in action, no one was about to challenge their leadership of the gang. To reinforce their authority, they held kangaroo courts in the snooker room at night. Those accused of overstepping had to appear. The evidence against them was recited. They then were given a chance to speak up in their defence. Then the judgement was given and the punishment handed out – a fine, a beating or expulsion from the gang.

What worried me about Mick was his growing collection of weaponry. He would scour antiques shop for bayonets, cavalry sabres, Samurai swords, machetes, anything menacing with a blade. It was his weekly task to sharpen them.

Then there were the guns. Mick would take me back to his flat to show off his arsenal which included a Walther PPK and a Beretta – who did he think was? James Bond? Then there was an antique Mauser, a new Luger automatic and a number of sawn-off shotguns. Nobody was in any doubt that he was itching for an excuse to use any or all of these.

While Mick concerned himself with his swords and guns, Steve concentrated on making money. Even the snooker hall was turning a profit. Despite the brothers' growing reputation for trouble, the place was attracting new customers. They were largely wide boys who fancied themselves as gangsters. The snooker hall provided a safe haven for would-be hoodlums, but the brothers made sure that there was no trouble there – except of their own making.

Young hoods could come there, drink and relax. They could talk openly about their plans and exploits. No one would dare grass. Steve maintained some contacts in the police via Dad's mates from the old days, so there was no chance that the cozzers could put an undercover cop in there – at least, not without our knowledge. And if the brothers knew about them, they wouldn't have lasted long.

People would not be allowed to settle old scores there. Those had to be taken outside if it was just a matter of fisticuffs. Anything more serious had to be taken to someone else's manor. Neither Mick nor Steve were keen on attracting police attention. If there was going to be a murder, they did not want the body on their doorstep. There were also informal patrols around nearby blocks to keep street crime down. The residents were grateful for the absence of vandalism and petty thievery, and local shopkeepers made their contribution to the fighting fund whether they wanted to or not.

With a secure base, regulars could leave their 'tools' on the premises, along with any valuable goods, safe in the knowledge that no one would nick them. The drugs came later. From Dad's generation, the brothers had inherited the old-fashioned code of crime. Protection, extortion, burglary, robbery, illegal gambling and the like were all on the cards; prostitution, people trafficking and drugs, back then, were not. All that would change when police successes in some areas of crime fighting would force us into new enterprises that guaranteed more rewards with fewer risks.

For the moment, the snooker hall worked as an introduction agency for criminals who wanted to do business with each other. Steve would use his contacts in exchange for a slice of any action. He could arrange transport, finance, fencing and, if muscle was needed, Mick could provide it.

Steve developed his hustle into a comprehensive service. There could be a nightwatchman at a warehouse who was in debt to the bookies and needed to get some heavy debt collectors off his back. The necessary cash would be forthcoming if he turned a blind eye. Steve would arrange a break-in with a truck ready to take the stolen goods away and line up customers to take the loot off the robbers' hands, with a backhander for ourselves, of course. Soon these casual arrangements turned into a full-blown criminal organisation.

And that, of course, began to step on other people's toes. There was a bunch in Tottenham based on the Broadwater Farm Estate. They called themselves the Farm Boys, while we disrespectfully called them the Seven Sisters. Apparently, they thought our activities were encroaching on their territory, so they called us out.

This was done in the old-fashioned manner. They invited the brothers for a drink on a Sunday morning in a pub in Finsbury Park to talk things over and settle the matter. The pub they picked was ostensibly a neutral venue, but was in fact Tottenham territory. Clearly this was not going to be a cosy chat over a couple of jars and a pint of whelks, regular Sunday lunchtime fare. It was going to be a face-off. And it was not just the two principal parties involved. The matter had been broadcast on the grapevine so that the whole of criminal London knew about it. There could only be one winner.

The Farm Boys were run by three ex-amateur heavy-weight boxers who took no lip. They figured that they were not about to be challenged by a couple of lightweight new-comers. As everyone knew about the meet, the brothers could not back down. If they did not turn up, their reputation would be blown and everyone would think they could walk all over them.

The challenge was the sole topic of conversation in the snooker hall – outside the brothers' hearing, of course. That Sunday morning, there was a record turnout. Everyone wanted to know how the brothers were going to handle it.

Mick had been out drinking the night before and he turned up unshaven and unusually dishevelled. Steve was immaculately dressed as usual but, incongruously, doing a little carpentry to fix the shelving behind the bar. Mick made everyone some tea. Nothing was said.

Steve had bought a Wolseley which he thought made him look like a respectable businessman. (Mick was more of a Jag man like Uncle Jack, back in the day.) Determined to make me pay my way, Steve decided that I should be his chauffeur. Of course, I had to do this the proper way, with a driving licence and insurance – things that Steve and Mick seldom bothered about. That meant a quick, intensive, two-week course at the British School of Motoring. When it came to the test, I'm not sure that cash did not change hands.

In those days, the pubs still opened at 12 noon on a Sunday. At 11.30, Steve told me to bring the Wolseley round and Steve and Mick headed off with me at the wheel. When we got to the pub in Finsbury Park, I was told to wait in the car outside. Steve and Mick went in alone. I was told the tale when I was driving them home.

Inside, apparently, the three top Farm Boys were waiting. One offered Steve and Mick a drink. They accepted. They were given a half of shandy each – a deliberate insult.

'That's what you little boys drink, isn't it,' they were told.

It was enough to kick things off. The barroom was already cleared and the bar staff fled, leaving them to get on with it. After twenty minutes or so, Steve and Mick emerged leaving a bar full of blood and broken glass. Two of the Farm Boys were out cold on the floor. Mick had to be dragged off the other one before he killed him.

# CHAPTER FOUR
## THE MANOR

Having established our patch against all comers, there was still the bread-and-butter work of being a criminal to do. It was taken for granted that the guv'nor of the manor was due what the Sicilian Mafia colourfully call the *pizzo* – which means a wetting of the beak. In other words, pubs, clubs, cafes, shopkeepers, betting shops and other businesses should all make their contribution for protection against other gangs. If some criminals came round causing trouble, we would sort it out. With Mick on hand, lesser crooks knew to stay away.

It was not punitive, only costing a business a few quid a week. Or there could be some other informal arrangement. Silver-tongued Steve would accept, shall we say, a loan or line of credit that would never get paid off. It was a matter of diplomacy. No one needed to get hurt. It was no great shakes, but it provided the brothers with a regular income.

The best pickings, of course, came from other criminals. Illegal gambling joints, unlicensed clubs, brothels and chop shops, where stolen cars are cut up to sell off the parts, were all fair game. After all, they could hardly go to the cops to complain. That meant Steve could up the punter's contribution when he felt like it. And no one in the manor would be working any of these rackets without our – that is his – knowledge, or our (his) say-so.

The snooker hall was a hub of intelligence. Most of the information came for free from the gossip of the guys who hung out there. Others sought to curry favour by dishing the dirt. Then there were barmen, taxi drivers and fences who would get paid for a tip-off. Steve made sure they got their whack if their lead checked out. The brothers also had a sixth sense. All three of us had lived in the area all our lives. We knew the game and little escaped our notice.

If some criminal on our patch pulled off a lucrative burglary or a tasty blag, it would be hard to keep it quiet. The local paper might carry a story. One of Dad's police informants might give Steve a nod. The word would spread. The culprit would then be invited to the snooker hall to discuss the brothers' percentage.

There were all sorts of other scams and cons going on. Pornography was another growth industry back then. Banned books, magazines and films were smuggled in from Denmark, Sweden and Germany to be sold in the sleazy bookshops in Soho and distributed around the country. The Metropolitan Police were notoriously bent at the time and they had to get their cut. They might also be persuaded to hand over material they seized at a suitable discount.

Then there was the constant use of violence. Steve and, particularly, Mick loved it. I wanted no part in it. Maybe I was just a wimp. And the way things were going, I could tell that trouble was brewing.

It came to a head one day after one of our mob had knocked over a print shop in Shepherd's Bush that was forging fivers and nicked £10,000 worth of them. The Bush was disputed territory between us and an up-and-coming Polish gang from Acton run by, of all people, Voytek from school.

Steve said he could get him the snide fivers back, but we needed our cut and suggested that they went fifty–fifty. Passing a large amount of dodgy currency is a risky business. But a dud fiver could be sold on for thirty bob (thirty shillings or £1.50 in new money), so they'd need to ante up £1,500 each. Voytek was dubious, but Steve persuaded him that half of something was better than nothing.

Voytek then wanted to know how good the notes were. Steve said they appeared perfect, indistinguishable from the real thing. It seemed his word was not good enough. Voytek wanted to see a sample. This pissed Steve off.

He arranged to meet Voytek in a cafe in White City. Steve took Lanky Pete with him, a guy who had done so much stir that he had lost his nerve but could still be useful as a dogsbody. Pete was introduced as the man who had done the blag on the forger.

At the cafe, Steve bought some teas and paid with a fiver. The woman behind the counter examined it suspiciously. Steve insisted he had nothing smaller. She finally accepted it and gave him his change.

That should have been good enough, but Voytek wanted to see another one. At the table, Pete showed Voytek another one, pulling it off a stout roll of fivers. Examining it closely, Voytek said it looked and felt real. So it should. Steve had got the fivers from the Barclays Bank in Notting Hill Gate that very morning.

Voytek had parked his car outside. It was a rather flashy Rover. They drove to Pete's flat off Harrow Road to get the dodgy notes. Parking in a road on the corner, Voytek went to get out of the car. Pete asked if it would be okay if he went in alone to get the goods on his own. He said that his wife did not know what he had been up to. She was afraid that if he was involved in crime again he would go back to prison, so he'd rather she did not know. In fact, Pete's old lady had left him years before, but Voytek wasn't to know that.

So Steve and Voytek sat in the car while Pete went round the corner to his flat. As soon as Pete got inside, he called 999, gave his address and asked them to send a squad car as a man was murdering his wife in the flat below.

A couple of minutes later, he came back around the corner carrying a large brown-paper parcel tied up with string. Steve had his £1,500 in his hand. Voytek did the same. Pete handed over the parcel. All that they had to do now was examine the contents.

Steve struggled with untying the string. It was tightly knotted. When he had removed the wrapping, he found another parcel inside. Just then, they heard the wail of a police siren and saw flashing blue lights. It seemed they had been rumbled.

Pete grabbed the door handle, ready to make a run for it. Steve said: 'Don't forget your money.' He grabbed the £1,500 from Voytek's hand and hand it over along with his own. Pete then jumped out and bolted.

As the squad car screeched to a halt, Voytek thought better of it and took off. As they were passing Shepherd's Bush station, Steve asked Voytek to let him out there. He had a business meeting he had to attend and he would take the underground.

Now they had done business together, Steve said he was sure he could trust Voytek with the dodgy notes. They could meet up later to divvy up. Honour among thieves and all that. They shook hands and parted with, presumably, Voytek figuring he'd got one over on Steve. No chance. It was only when Voytek got home and opened the parcel that he discovered that the parcel was full of neatly guillotined newspaper that I'd spent all morning cutting up. Pete, of course, handed over the £3,000 to Steve and got £100 for his trouble.

Steve related this story with relish. I was not so sure about it. After all, I had been at school with Voytek. We had not exactly been mates, but he had never given me any trouble. I just didn't like swindling people I knew. Besides, if I knew Voytek, he wouldn't leave it there.

Indeed, he did not. He sent a henchman named Tomasz Nowak to the snooker hall armed with a loaded shotgun and asking for Steve. I was there and there was an unpleasant scene. When Tomasz found Steve, he wished he hadn't. He was beaten up and dumped in the street, still clutching his shooter. The police found him there and he was arrested. Charged with carrying a loaded firearm, he was fined £50. Needless to say, Voytek and his bunch of Poles were not best pleased with us. Worse was to come.

The attack on the snooker hall narked Mick. He headed for Acton and walked into the Polish club that Voytek used as his headquarters. This was deliberate provocation. Voytek was not there, but someone must have called him. Soon he and three other Poles in Voytek's Rover were heading down the road towards the club. They were tooled up. But Mick was way ahead of them. He had heavily armed soldiers in two cars at the end of the street.

As the Rover approached, it was peppered with bullets. Voytek screeched to a halt and jammed the car into reverse as his boys returned fire. They sped off spraying the area with bullets. It was a miracle that no one was hit.

Despite the ruckus, the police were nowhere to be seen. They only turned up later when residents complained of broken windows and bullet holes in their walls. At first, the police could not be bothered to investigate the incident. Perhaps they thought it was a good idea for two mobs to wipe each other out in a Western-style shoot-'em-up. But when the press got involved, they were forced to act.

Some local worthy had taken down the registration number of Voytek's car. In the Old Bailey, he pleaded guilty to violent behaviour and got thirty months – time he spent nurturing a lifelong resentment towards my brothers and the snooker hall crew.

# CHAPTER FIVE
## GOING STRAIGHT

The shoot-up in Acton was the last straw for me. I didn't want a life of crime. The last thing I wanted was to spend years in prison like Dad. I'd seen him inside a jail for myself, heard about the stuff he'd had to put up with and so it was no surprise that he had aged prematurely. Now in his mid-forties, he could have been sixty.

The way Steve and Mick were going had no appeal either. Sooner or later they were going to get a bullet in the head, be cut to pieces or end up in a concrete pillar in the extension of Westway, which was then being built. Besides, all that ducking and diving was just too much hard work. You were always looking over your shoulder. Cheating and stealing was not really a sustainable lifestyle. It always catches up with you in the end, or so I thought back then.

I had been a bit young during the hippy era of the sixties when everyone lauded the outsider. Who didn't want to be an *Easy Rider*? The film *Bonnie and Clyde* hero-worshipped two bank robbers and look what happened to them. Mick Jagger played an outlaw in *Ned Kelly* and messes with crooks in Notting Hill Gate in *Performance*. In neither case does it turn out well.

Then there was *The Godfather* in 1972 (though I had read the book beforehand), but that was the US, and we didn't have criminal dynasties in the UK to prove that it worked. The Krays produced no progeny to take over their firm, except for Charlie who may have had a daughter, while the twins themselves never saw daylight again.

I guess I was a little too old for punk. My brothers kept me well funded through the 1970s recession, so I was never dole fodder. The lifestyle of that generation had little appeal. Just think of what happened to Sid Vicious.

Then I was in my mid-twenties when Thatcher came to power. It was time to take life seriously. If I was not going to be dragged into full-time criminality, then I was in danger of being stuck as a barman all my life. What I needed was some of the education that I had thrown away so carelessly when I was a teenager.

I read a lot, but I still couldn't imagine trying to make it as a writer. There would be no starving in a garret for me. My brothers would always be there dragging me back into the business. I would never be able to break free.

With Thatcher in power, the word of the moment was 'monetarism' and I did understand a bit about money. I'd seen enough pass through the snooker hall – over the counter in the bar, under the counter for dodgy gear, nicked and fake. What's more I had a passing grade in O level maths.

I was still in touch with Terry and Curtis though they had moved out of the area. They had passed their A levels and gone on to university. Terry had studied computer science at Exeter and was now a programmer. Curtis had read economics and was working as a trader in the City.

Although they were encouraging, there was no way I was going to get into university, but Terry said he had heard of a college in Camden that might be a good bet. So I got in touch and went along for an open day. They had a course on accounting and payroll. I was good at arithmetic. Curtis said it wasn't exactly economics, but it was a start. From there I could qualify in accountancy. At the time, being a chartered accountant was a bit of a joke, but he explained there was a career path. Everyone needed accountants. There were huge accountancy firms in the City. It was an international business.

There were also rumours that Thatcher was planning a 'Big Bang', deregulating the markets and throwing open the financial sector. The old men with bowler hats were going to be put out to grass and a new generation of younger whizz-kids were going to be brought in. While I did not see myself as a whizz-kid – and, I mean, I wasn't that young any more – the idea seemed exciting and like a way ahead.

Of course, my dad didn't like the sound of it. He thought that I ought to stay with the family, but some of the old lags like Lanky Pete who knew him said I ought to get out while

I could. They, too, had spent too long in jail and didn't think I should go that way.

Mum, naturally, was supportive of anything I wanted to do. She never asked what Steve and Mick got up to, but felt instinctively that it was something unsavoury. Her thoughts were that it was best that I steered clear of it. I was still her mummy's boy.

And I was still 'little brother' to Steve and Mick. They said they would stand by me whatever I wanted to do. But they didn't understand why I would opt for such a boring life as being an accountant. How could I choose the nine-to-five life instead of the exciting existence they offered? There was the thrill of outsmarting the police and facing down rival gangs. There was easy money. You could stay in bed all day and the suckers under your protection still paid up, and members of the snooker crew, if they did a little freelance work, would feel obligated to cut you in without even being asked. It was cushty.

Was it birds I was worried about? Did I want to go to college because I fancied getting off with lots of students? But plenty of good-looking bints turned up at the snooker hall every time we had a party. That was true enough. I don't want to sound too prudish; they weren't tarts exactly, but they were good-time girls. They were only too keen to hang around anyone who had money.

Not that I was still a virgin. I'd had my share. It was easy, but I don't want to go into that. A gentleman should not kiss and tell. Let's say, I had cash and they weren't the sort of girls you took home to Mother. Steve and Mick certainly did not take any of them home. Mum and Dad were from a different generation. Back then it was okay for a man to fool around, but a girl needed to keep herself, well, special. Free love had yet to come to the lower classes.

If I was going to lead a straight life, I was going to need a wife and kids, and I certainly wasn't going to find a wife I could build a life with anywhere near the snooker hall. I figured I could do better. So I signed up for the course in accounting and payroll with the college. Camden was far enough away for my brothers' reputation not to have spread to the average Joe on the street. Even in Kensal Town I had kept myself out of the limelight. Besides, the other students came from all over London, some even further afield, so they knew nothing of our Firm.

I approached my first day with some trepidation. I always imagined students to be nice middle-class kids who would be in their late teens and early twenties. In other words, much younger than me. And they would be smart.

This wasn't the case. Some were younger, but had mucked up at school and were out for a second chance. Others were older, seeking to take courses and get new qualifications so they could change direction later in life. Then there were the real oldies who, I guess, were just taking courses to pass the time. Thankfully, there were plenty of women. And not the type you find hanging out around the snooker halls.

Not only was there a range of ages among the students, it was the same among the teachers. Some were older than me, some younger. It was one of the teachers that caught my eye, an olive-skinned brunette who I learned later was called Victoria – or rather Vittoria.

# CHAPTER SIX
## VITTORIA

Again, that is not her real name, but I wanted something very Spanish. Because she is Spanish and it plays a significant part in my story. She was the daughter of a man who had fought in the Spanish Civil War on the Republican side and fled to France when General Franco took over as dictator in 1937. Even though he had fought against the Fascist Falange, when World War II started two years later, he was interned. Having declared war on Hitler's Germany, the French had no wish to antagonise Franco, so tried to persuade the refugees to return to Spain. Vittoria's father knew what he could expect at Franco's hands. He escaped and made it to England where, as a foreign national, he joined the Pioneer Corps.

After World War II, he naturalised as a British subject and became a successful businessman. He married Vittoria's mum, a translator who had read Spanish and French at St Hilda's College, Oxford. They had a son, who I shall call Alejandro (Alexander to his friends), and, sometime later, a daughter. They had been born here and Vittoria was British as well as being fiercely proud of her Spanish heritage.

Now, this is not a love story. It is supposed to be my story of being a crime lord and how I became one. So I will keep the details to a minimum. It is traditional that mob bosses keep their personal life out of the business, but in my case my relationship with Vittoria plays a vital part of the story as she was another reason I wanted to stay out of the world of crime. Nevertheless, I failed in that ambition, and regrettably she became inextricably mixed up in it.

So yes, I met her at college. I was a student, she was a teacher, teaching Spanish and ESOL – English for Speakers of Other Languages. These days, relationships between teachers and pupils are disapproved of. Back then it was different. Alongside my accounting course, I signed up to study Spanish, just to be in her class. I should point out that I was two years older than her. We were both over twenty-one so there was nothing criminal going on, unlike other parts of my life.

To give myself pocket money while I was a student, I continued working shifts behind the bar at the snooker hall, and this meant I had the cash to take her out.

Clearly, as she was a teacher and had been to university, she was much better educated than me. She had a BA (Hons) degree in English Literature from University College London, so we had a love of books in common. Strangely, even though I had just read anything that took my fancy while she had read in a structured way to fulfil the syllabus, there were lots of books we had both read. She recommended other titles to fill gaps in my education, while I could offer her others that would never have made the curriculum. She'd never read James Bond. Never mind her intellectual stuff, I wish I could write the seamless prose of Ian Fleming.

The problem was when it came to family. Naturally, I was very guarded about my background. She knew I was from a working-class area, but I had been to grammar school, which was a plus. I told her about my mother and the tough life she had had, but could hardly tell her that my dad had been in and out of jail. She must've got the impression that I was brought up by a single mum. And my brothers may as well not have existed as I made no mention of them. I did tell her I worked in a bar to finance my belated education, but she didn't know whom the bar belonged to.

It was probably clear I was holding back, which is why she only gave me the broadest description of her own clan. It seems that her father had been alienated from the rest of his family who had supported Franco during the Civil War. Similarly, her mother had been cut off from her family in the north when she went to Oxford. And after that, she'd done the unthinkable. She had married a foreigner and a Catholic to boot.

In a very Spanish way, Vittoria's family was very important to her and she was fiercely protective of them. They lived out in Surrey and she would visit most weekends, usually on a Sunday. But being very British too, she had moved to London and shared a flat with two other girls when she went to UCL. Now that she had a job, she could afford a flat on her own.

As I was still living in Portland Road, I could hardly take her home, so our relationship, as it rapidly became, was largely conducted in her apartment. This suited us both and it gave her the opportunity to give me a thorough education in middle-class ways. She was a teacher both in college and at home.

We did all the usual things middle-class people do: we went to restaurants, the cinema, the theatre and, sometimes, out shopping together on a Saturday, though I balked when she suggested that we visit the antiques market in Portobello Road, in case we bumped into someone I knew. I would probably have risked going to the Notting Hill Carnival, but she never asked.

Although I had only taken the Spanish course to have an opportunity to meet her, I had fallen into my own trap. She liked to speak Spanish at home, as she had with her parents, and I struggled to keep up. In the end, though, it would be worth the effort.

Having an artistic bent, she took little interest in accountancy but, as a teacher, she made me stick to my studies. We both knew that, if we were going to make a go of it, me getting qualifications in accountancy was going to be the way ahead. If I failed and slipped back to life in W10, I could hardly have taken her with me. Life in the ghetto, as it was then, would not have suited her. And I didn't want to go back there either. Apart from my bar shifts, it was a life that I was still struggling to leave behind.

My accountancy and bookkeeping courses only lasted a year and I passed with flying colours. I signed up with the Institute of Chartered Accountants to continue my studies. Then, after more exams, I would be able to work in my new-found profession. I also continued my Spanish courses, simply to keep up with the conversation at home. It's not giving much away to say that Spanish is a very romantic language, so it kinda suited the mood of the moment.

After about a year together, Vittoria and I decided that we needed a holiday. The destination was to be Spain. The old dictator General Franco was dead, democracy was slowly being restored and Vittoria wanted to explore her heritage. So no package holiday on the Costa Brava for us.

I had planned to fly out there, hire a car and drive around, but Steve would not have it. Instead, he bought us an MGB, a classic British soft-top sports car. It was the perfect way to travel around the countryside and cities of the Iberian Peninsula. It went like the wind and gave you an all-round view. The idea was that we should take the car ferry to Calais and drive down through France and over the Pyrenees.

It was to be my first time abroad and I had to get a

passport. There was all sorts of paperwork concerning the car to sort out as well. Then we headed off.

We took a leisurely drive down through France via Le Mans, Poitiers, Bordeaux and Toulouse, stopping at small hotels along the way. Crossing the Pyrenees through Andorra, we headed for the coast.

That night in Barcelona, Vittoria and I were dining in a restaurant when we began discussing what our future together might be. As we had been a couple for over a year now, it was clear that we were pretty serious about each other. Vittoria had no great ambitions. She was happy being a teacher but did, ultimately, want to get married and have children.

I was all for that. It was what I wanted too, but not until I got my foot on the first step of the career ladder. It would still be some time before I would be fully qualified as an accountant and only then would I be able to get a mortgage and buy a house for us that would be big enough to bring up children in. She was happy with that as a long-term plan but said she needed some sort of commitment.

She explained that in Spanish culture, family was very important and she was going to prove it to me. While her father had been alienated from his family during the Spanish Civil War, he had not cut off all connection and had given Vittoria their addresses. As she was going to Spain, he thought she should visit them.

Her aunt and several cousins lived in Málaga – Andalusia had been a stronghold of Franco's Falangists, hence their alienation from Vittoria's father. We drove down there along the coast. The family were welcoming. Her cousins were in business. They joked about the 'Costa del Crime' – so-called because of the number of British criminals who had made their home along the Costa del Sol. Vittoria's cousins welcomed the amount of money that these Brits had brought with them. It had apparently done wonders for the local economy and business had flourished.

The family wined and dined us, and showed us the sights. After ten days, we said *adiós* and headed back north. One night we were having a drink in Cordoba when she pointed out that now I knew a lot about her family. There were no secrets. She had been very open. But, she said, she knew practically nothing about mine. Why was I being so secretive?

Perhaps it was the wine. I was relaxed. It was a warm evening in a foreign country. The holiday, so far, had been full of love. Maybe this was the time to come clean.

I refilled our glasses. Then I took the plunge. Dad, I explained, had been a career criminal who had been in and out of jail. I told her about my prison visits as a child. I said that Dad had retired now, at least from that life, but my brothers were a different matter. With little parental control they had run wild and were now full-time gangsters.

I reckoned that it was only a matter of time before they ended up shot dead or in jail.

I told her that I was determined not to follow them down that route. I had seen enough of the life of crime – the petty vendettas, the random violence, the worship of money over all other considerations, the callous disregard for the interests of others, the insides of prisons and the toll it took on family life.

I wanted what she wanted – a house, kids, a comfortable life with no worries or stress. I did not want to be looking over my shoulder all the time to see if the cops were on my trail or someone was coming to kill me. That was not the life for me.

That was why I had gone to college to study accountancy – the most boring, steady and respectable profession imaginable. Since I had met her, I had redoubled my determination to succeed in that modest goal. If she did not mind having a boring life somewhere in the suburbs, then I was hers. She said that it need not be that boring. We could find exciting things to do and we laughed about the idea of me learning to play golf while she made jam.

But there was a lot to consider. Was that really the life we wanted? For me, cleaning the car on a Sunday morning and taking the kids to football practice seemed like heaven on earth, especially if she was waiting for me when I got back from work. But she had a broader education. I was not sure that being a housewife would be enough for her. It is difficult to see inside someone else's head, and I had no idea what was in hers. This was in the early 1980s and second-wave feminism had not reached the high-water mark it has now. Looking back, I guess I was a bit sexist.

For the next few days, as we drove across Spain's central plateau, Vittoria was silent. Clearly, she had a lot to think about. The only topics of conversation were where we were going to stop for lunch, whether we were coming up to a town where there would be a good hotel and what we were going to have for dinner. Small talk.

In Madrid, we visited the Prado. Vittoria was into art and again wanted to relish her Spanish heritage. I considered this part of my education. If we were going to be together, I had better learn to enjoy art too.

Passing back into France, our holiday was drawing to a close and still there were things unspoken between us. We stopped off in Paris, but it was not until we spent our last night in Amiens that Vittoria took me by the hand and told me that she must meet my family. If I showed them that we were together, she would consider that a commitment. After all, if we were to be married, she would be part of the family.

I had my misgivings, but I realised that if I didn't agree, I would lose her and, if I lost her, I might slip back into the murky world of crime from which I was only just emerging. I said that I would make arrangements to take her to Notting Hill to meet Mum and Dad. Perhaps even Uncle Jack. But I thought that we should leave the introduction to Steve and Mick until another time. I didn't say it, but I thought: possibly never.

Vittoria was delighted, though she wasn't prepared to reciprocate in terms of me meeting her parents – not yet, at least. She thought that it would be best if we put off introducing me to them until I had passed my AAT Level 4 and had a secure job in accountancy. Her dad was an old-fashioned Spaniard. He was very protective of his daughter. Any prospective son-in-law would be thoroughly vetted. He must have a respectable profession and be able, as they say, to keep his daughter in the style that she had become accustomed to. He must have changed a great deal from the rebellious left-wing student prepared to take up arms to protect the Republic in his youth.

True to my word, when we got back to England, I phoned Mum and Dad and told them that I wanted to bring Vittoria over to meet them. Mum was delighted. She said they would have a barbecue in the back garden. It was late September but the weather was still nice. She would invite the brothers, Uncle Jack, the neighbours, some of Dad's friends. My heart sank.

No, Mum, I said, I'd seen the forecast. The weather was about to turn. And Vittoria, I said, was rather shy (which wasn't the case at all). It would be better if we came over one evening for dinner, just the four of us. Vittoria could meet Steve and Mick on another occasion. 'Yes, dear,' Mum said.

The following Thursday we went over and introductions were made. It was rather awkward at first, but Mum asked Vittoria whether she would like to see around the house. I was left to talk to Dad, who could only ask how I was doing before the phone rang. It was Steve. Mick was with him. Why hadn't they been invited, they wanted to know. Then they wanted to speak to me and began to take the piss out of me and my girl. Was she too posh to mix with the likes of them? I told them that she certainly was a cut above the slappers they hung out with and put the phone down.

The tour of the house was over and Vittoria was very impressed. She loved the way that Mum had done it out and it was even bigger than the house that her parents had out in Surrey. She seemed surprised. She did not say anything about the area of London it was in and its shady reputation. But then she didn't know what a slum it had been when I was growing up. Now, it was well on its way to gentrification.

Mum talked about the old times and how much better it was today. And, yes, the house was big. In fact, too big for her to cope with. They didn't need such a big place. I rarely made an appearance there, and Steve and Mick had also made other arrangements. They were old enough to take care of themselves anyway. She and Dad had been talking about retiring to the south coast. She mentioned Bexhill-on-Sea where she had once gone on a day trip. A friend had moved down there and said it was nice. Dad put his oar in, saying that most of his mates had retired out in southern Spain. Even Vittoria knew he was referring to the Costa del Crime.

Mum was not keen, though. She said she could never get used to all those funny foreign ways. Then she turned, flustered, to Vittoria, touched her on the hand and said, 'Sorry, dear.' Vittoria said it was quite all right. No offence. After all, she came from Surrey.

Eventually, a lot of Dad's old pals were kicked out of Spain, while I, as a mob boss, would eventually follow them into exile.

# ACT II

## DAYLIGHT ROBBERY

1982–95

# CHAPTER SEVEN
## ACROSS THE PAVEMENT

The meeting with Mum and Dad seemed to have done the trick with Vittoria. Clearly, she could see that I was proud of her and had, at last, shown commitment. She mentioned the lovely house that my parents had several times. But there was no mention of the idea that it came from the spoils of crime. Perhaps she thought that it had been bought with the proceeds of the various crimes my father had committed and that it was fine because he had now paid his debt to society with his long years in jail. But Dad had never had that sort of money. The money had come from the current crimes of my brothers who had no intention of doing time for their crimes.

Still having my studies to complete, I went back to work behind the bar in the snooker hall. Steve upped my wages. He liked having me there. Any replacement risked disaster. If The Filth ever managed to put an undercover cop behind the bar, they'd all end up in jail.

While I had been working hard at my studies before our holiday, Steve and Mick had begun a new career. They had been 'going across the pavement'. That is, they had turned their hands to armed robbery, committing old-style bank robberies like it was the Wild West. All the crims were doing it, they said. Like the old robber Willie Sutton said: 'That's where the money is.' More than that, though, I think they got off on the excitement.

The key element here was, if possible, not to hurt anyone – just scare them. So one barrel of the sawn-off would be loaded with rice rather than shotgun pelts. If there was any resistance, the troublemaker would be blasted with rice. They would figure that they had been shot and would hit the deck, only to realise later that, apart from a bit of a sting and some bruising, they hadn't been wounded. It shut everyone else up though and it would increase the speed that the cashiers would empty their tills, so by the time everyone realised the person wasn't dead, my brothers would be long gone. Banks had a policy that allowed their staff to hand over the cash if their customers were directly threatened. If this ever didn't happen, Steve insisted that you should only shoot someone with your pistol, but only as a last resort and only if your liberty was on the line. Even if you fired, you should try not to kill anyone, particularly the Old Bill, unless you wanted to spend a very long time behind bars.

The truth is that most professional robbers are not out to kill or maim. They want easy money and know that they may have to do ruthless and horrible things to get it, but aren't drawn to violence. This is unlike other violent criminals, such as serial killers, sadistic sickos, knife-wielding rapists or football hooligans. Violence – or, rather, the threat of violence – for the armed robber is a necessity not a pleasure. The perfect armed robbery, from the perpetrators' point of view, would be to grab the loot and get clean away without anybody being physically hurt. Shooting people or injuring them during an armed robbery only motivates the police and gets the public spotlight on you. Rewards are offered and people are more likely to turn you in. It also adds more years to the already stiff sentence you'll get if you're caught and convicted. No criminal wants that.

Even so, committing armed robbery was not an occupation for the faint-hearted. It takes a whole lot of bottle to put yourself out there when you know that the end result could be a whole heap of years in prison. Rarely does a professional armed robber get less than double figures when it comes to sentencing.

And don't forget, your life is on the line too. The cozzers got tired of crooks hiring fancy lawyers, cooking up some snide alibi to con the jury and walking out of the court a free man. So if they got wind of a bank job, they would send out armed police to shoot anyone they saw in commission of an armed robbery. And the British police did not shoot to wound. They saw it as their duty to stop the criminal dead in his tracks. They shoot to kill. There is a long list of armed robbers who have been shot dead by the police. The cops see it as a bonus. It limits the number of career criminals on the street and cuts the future crime figures.

It was no secret to the blaggers that the Flying Squad – aka SO7 or The Sweeney – had introduced a shoot-to-kill policy. In the long history of the Metropolitan Police, no officer has ever faced prosecution over these extra-judicial killings. Even the slaying of Brazilian electrician Jean Charles de Menezes after the 7/7 bombings in 2005 went unpunished.

In 1983, three cops fired fourteen rounds into 26-year-old film editor Stephen Waldorf, mistaking him for an escaped criminal. Five bullets hit. One of the cops then pointed his gun at Waldorf between the eyes and pulled the trigger. But he was out of bullets, so he pistol-whipped the innocent man instead.

No charges were brought against one of the cozzers and the other two went to trial, but were acquitted after claiming they were genuinely afraid of an unarmed man. No disciplinary proceedings were taken against them. If that was not enough, the Police Federation asked that, in future, firearm officers should be given a degree of legal immunity.

Steve had done his research and said you never knew when armed policemen were coming out of the woodwork. No matter how much you cased a joint, there could always be some cozzers lurking. There was always a chance that someone had grassed you up, so the Old Bill was on to you. Another team could've taken a fancy to the same target bank and the police could've staked out the place hoping to nab them.

Nevertheless, with Steve's eye for detail and meticulous planning, the boys usually got away with it. Once the job was done, they'd be back across the pavement and into the get-away car in less than four minutes all told. One of the team would do a countdown during the operation. The stolen car would speed off, then, once out of sight, slow down to attract less attention.

The car they used would be stolen to order. You need a regular four-door family saloon. Nothing sporty or beat up, so it would not stand out or be in any way memorable. A Vauxhall Astra was a favourite. It was the perfect car for robberies. There were so many of them on the streets that, unless the car was bright pink or dayglo orange, it could blend in very nicely with other traffic. A getaway car didn't have to be supercharged or souped up as there really was no great need for speed; it is more about anonymity than speed and power when it comes to getaway cars. The two things you wanted from a getaway car were that it worked reliably and didn't stand out and attract attention.

Steve had a specialist motor man who largely nicked cars from the car parks of railway stations in the commuter belt. He went there mid-morning when you could practically guarantee that he wouldn't be disturbed by the owner returning. They would have taken the train to work or to make a shopping trip to town and wouldn't be back to collect the car until mid-afternoon at the earliest.

His technique was simple. He would insert the blade of a large pair of medical scissors into the lock and jiggle it up and down. It would only take a few seconds. Once the lock was sprung, the car alarm would sound. That didn't matter. No one took any notice of an alarm in the daytime, unless it was a fire alarm. The only person who would respond to a car alarm was the owner and they would have gone off on the train and be miles away. Otherwise, the alarm would only sound for a minute or two.

Once inside the car, Steve's guy would screw a self-tapping screw into the ignition until it was tight. He then went to work with a heavyweight slide-hammer, jerking it hard. If the lock was stubborn, he would jerk it a couple of times more, then the whole ignition lock would pop out of its barrel. Once the lock had been removed, he stuck a large flat-headed screwdriver into the empty barrel and twisted it. This would turn the alarm off. Everyone's heard a car alarm go off down the street, then stop after a minute or so. It happens all the time. No one gives it any notice. The engine would then start up and he was good to go.

The day before a job, he would nick two cars, hiding them

overnight in a rented garage. In the morning, one car – the changeover car – would be parked in a quiet street not far from the target bank. The other one would be used for the actual blag. Once the job was done, the getaway car would park around the corner from the changeover car. It would be left there in case it had been spotted at the job and reported to the police.

By the time they reached the changeover, the robbers would have packed up the cash and guns in anonymous holdalls. They would carry these around the corner to the changeover car. With luck there would be no one around to see this. If there was, they'd only see a couple of men getting out of one car or a couple of men getting into another car. With care, they wouldn't see both and there would be no link between the two motors. They would drive to a safe house to divvy up the loot. The changeover car would be dumped and the crooks would drive home in their own, legally owned motors.

The same crash-bang hold-up technique worked on jewellers and branches of Thomas Cook, the travel agents, which carried large stocks of travellers' cheques and foreign currencies. According to the newspapers, back then, armed robberies took place, on average, once every five days in London. Millions of pounds were going missing and my brothers were getting their share.

Once they'd pulled off a heist, they would skip the

country for a few weeks. Before they started off, they'd already have a plane ticket to Torremolinos in their pocket. The mantra was 'sawn-off shotgun on the streets of London at lunchtime, sawn-off shorts on the beach in Spain at teatime'.

Of course, the powers that be decided that something had to be done about this. Banks and jewellers, anywhere handling valuables, installed bulletproof screens and panic buttons under the counter connected direct to the nearest police station. The police upped their budget to pay informants and the era of the 'supergrass' began.

Clearly the Met knew what we were up to, but Steve planned the raids so well that the dicks could never find any evidence. However, as I was one of the family and behind the bar in the snooker hall, they must have figured that I knew something. I was the weakest link so I began to get visits. There was no point in trying to bribe me, but they could put the pressure on. I was an accessory and, unless I turned Queen's evidence (as it was then) and testified for the prosecution, I would face a long time in jail. Although that's what I dreaded, you don't grass. And you don't grass on your family. I guess, if they went down, I did too.

Eventually, SmartWater was introduced. Above the door of any likely target for a blag there would be a canister. This would be activated from behind the counter and spray an indelible infra-red liquid dye on the would-be robber. It would stain the blagger's clothing and the skin for weeks. Later, each batch of SmartWater contained a DNA marking that was unique to each premises. Once you felt the cooling spray from above, it was time to get out of there. The Old Bill would be on their way. Then you would have to ditch your clothes and stay out of circulation, basically sitting in a shower for a month until it wore off.

By then, going across the pavement didn't seem such an attractive proposition any more. The idea now was to grab the money when it was outside the bank – on its way in or way out. The target would be the security vans that carried the cash. A team of two or three could knock over a bank or a jeweller's. Now what was needed was an altogether bigger operation.

While I had been away on holiday with Vittoria, Steve had been recruiting. He and Mick wanted to up their game and play for bigger stakes. The security vans that toured businesses collecting large amounts of cash and delivering payrolls on a Thursday or Friday were the obvious target. Back then, they were lightly protected with poorly paid security guards who could be easily intimidated.

They got in touch with one of the guys who pulled off the first ever security van heist back in 1968 in Shepherd's Bush. He had the necessary experience. Then he got a couple of 'technicians' (these were the men who actually unloaded the cash), while Mick and other heavies that Steve recruited waved their weapons in the air. They needed a wheelman. Steve found an ex-rally driver who had done a few getaways.

An arsenal of heavyweight weapons was required. After the war, there were plenty of guns about, but by the 1970s and 1980s it was hard to get your hands on them in the UK. So a break-in at a gun shop in Essex was organised. This yielded one Browning 12-bore semi-automatic shotgun, one Mossberg 12-bore shotgun, one Winchester 101 shotgun, one Manu-france Perfex semi-automatic 12-bore shotgun, one Manufrance 12-bore pump-action shotgun, one Remington pump-action shotgun and one Savage 12-bore shotgun. That was enough for the biggest job. Despite Steve's concern for security, Mick couldn't help showing these off in the bar of the snooker hall. He was over the moon.

While Mick was flashing his new toys around, Steve put together a hamper of silly disguises – false beards, outsized moustaches, ginger wigs and coloured glasses. Some of the gang were even willing to dress up as women to confuse witnesses.

You also needed a couple of amenable security guards who knew about procedures and schedules. Mick and his mate Chopper went to visit the family of a security driver. Suitably intimidated, he provided a rota of deliveries and pick-ups that would prove invaluable. Chopper met another security guard who worked for Group 4 through a mutual love of fishing. He provided more invaluable information.

The first robbery was carefully planned. It was to be pulled off inside the underpass at Hanger Lane where the security guards would not be able to use their old walkie-talkies as their signals would be blocked. A member of the team was dressed as a policeman and stopped the westbound traffic behind a large truck at the eastern end. Another stopped the security van carrying the payroll for Park Royal Industrial Estate inside the tunnel. At the same time, another guy skewed a stolen truck across the carriageway in, blocking the view from both ends. Another 'moody' policeman then confiscated the keys from backed-up motorists so they could not drive off and raise the alarm. All this had to be done with precision timing.

Three stolen cars and a stolen van, which had been following closely, surrounded the security van. The windscreen was smashed with an axe and the crew were faced with three men wielding sawn-offs. They offered no resistance and handed over the custodian's keys that gave access to the cash. The money was then transferred into the stolen van and the boys made off with some £100,000.

Within hours, the money was divided up in a flophouse – that is, a hideaway set up for the purpose. Then the robbers went their separate ways, not only richer but still pumped up with adrenaline. When they got back to the bar, they all talked about the buzz they got from such a blag. They said it was better than drugs. And then everyone would go into hiding, for a few months at least.

Not every job went so smoothly, though. The mob's next job was at a factory in Northolt. Again armed with shotguns, the team waited in two cars, but when the security van turned up it stopped at a delivery point that was three hundred yards from where the informant had said. The plan was simple: to hijack the security van. But by the time they had reached it, it had driven off.

So far, no one had got hurt. Not that anyone cared particularly, but if one of the guards got injured or killed there would be a lot more publicity and more heat from the police. The blaggers had depended on the security guards being so intimidated that they would simply hand over the custodian's keys. But what happened if one of them decided to be a hero?

Mick, with his usual flare for going over the top, came up with the answer. He had always been a fan of *The Texas Chainsaw Massacre*. The security vans back then were like sardine cans. The blade of a chainsaw would simply chew its way straight through the metal. The first outing was a failure as the chainsaw failed to fire up. It was electric, but no one had remembered to charge it up beforehand. Nevertheless, some mad gangster waving a chainsaw about was enough to give the security guards the shits and they handed the keys over anyway. Maybe they'd seen the film too.

The next plan really took my brothers' fancy. They had heard that at eleven o'clock on Tuesdays, a Security Express van carrying a large amount of cash left the Midland Bank in the High Street, Banstead, Surrey, where Steve and Mick had been in borstal ten years earlier. Mick always liked to be in on the action, but Steve usually confined himself to the planning. But this time he decided to go along too, for old times' sake.

Steve gave a final briefing to the nine-man team in an 'out', or safe house, in Kensal Rise on the morning of the robbery. They knew that the van was heading towards Sutton and, by means they wouldn't tell me, knew the back road it took. The gang left the flat separately at one-minute intervals heading for six stolen vehicles parked within a few hundred yards.

These formed up into a convoy and headed south, crossing the river over Battersea Bridge. Passing through Mitcham, they heard a siren. The driver of the lead car, which was carrying most of the blagging gear, saw the police car in his rear-view mirror and pulled over. He was bricking it. If the police searched the car, there was enough equipment in the boot to get him done for intending to carry out a robbery at the very least.

The rest of the team pulled up at a safe distance to watch what was going on. But the police car didn't stop. It sailed on by, presumably on another call-out, thinking nothing of the car that pulled over for them. It was a close call, but the team went on as planned.

They stopped in a small wood on Sutton Lane, a narrow wooded road less than a mile from my brothers' old digs in borstal. Ahead of schedule, they had plenty of time to get the motors in the right position for an ambush.

Two of the cars had gone ahead into Banstead village. They shadowed the security van from the bank on the High Street. On Sutton Lane, one car overtook the van then indicated that it was going to turn right, forcing the van to slow down. Then another car pulled out of the wood, stopping the traffic behind the van, so it could go neither forward nor back.

The gang's van emerged from the wood and stopped alongside the security van. Three men with shotguns jumped out and blew out the security van's tyres. This time, the chainsaw was charged and already warmed up. All the men wore masks and motorbike helmets to cover their faces, and had their hands covered with surgical gloves.

Steve was carrying a stopwatch. He had given the team just three minutes to pull off the hold-up, worrying that any longer would put them at risk. The cutter and the technicians were not even armed. They had other jobs to do. Our driver in the rear car was dressed in a police uniform to hold any traffic back.

The van driver and his mate were dragged out of their seats

on to the grass verge. When one of them moved, the gunmen let off a warning shot in the air. This didn't distract the man wielding the chainsaw. After ninety seconds, he was through and the technicians began bundling the sacks full of cash into the robbers' van.

With the three minutes up, Steve blew a whistle and shouted: 'Go! Go! Go!'

The van took off. The other men piled into three cars, leaving the cars that had been used in the heist behind. Following the van, they were careful not to exceed the 30mph speed limit. In the back of the van, the cash sacks were loaded into a plastic body bag with a zip up the front. There were forty of them containing £20,000 each.

Back in Kensal Rise, the body bag was carried into the 'out' where the £800,000 was divvied up. It was all done and dusted in twenty minutes. While I wasn't involved in the raid, I knew soon that they'd made a big hit. There was money flying over the bar and Steve gave me the nod and a pay rise. I pieced together the details later through loose talk in the sanctuary of the snooker hall.

The problem for me was that, by default, I was getting a masterclass in armed robbery. Sooner or later, the police would be turning up. And the boys in the gang were now hardened criminals. What would happen when one of them figured I knew too much?

# CHAPTER EIGHT
## SUNDAY LUNCH

It was 1982. I was twenty-six and was now a qualified accountant. Curtis asked around and got me an internship in a large
accountancy firm in the City. I won't name them for reasons
you will see later. Though I was not entirely unpaid, my salary
was less than my wages tending the bar in the snooker hall. I
was learning the trade, I was told. As a result, I continued
doing shifts in the bar, particularly at the weekends. Otherwise, we would have had to rely on Vittoria's income.

However, progress was being made. I was gainfully
employed with a salary that was declared to the Inland Revenue, and income tax was deducted at source (rather than
being paid in cash out of the till, which was not accounted
for). My employer promised me that, as I progressed in the
company, my salary would rise exponentially. They drew my
attention to the big bucks the top guys were making. One day
I may even be made a partner and take a share in the profits.
For the moment, though, an income from which I could
afford a mortgage was the only thing I had my sights on.

Vittoria and I had a little celebration on the day my first
salary cheque arrived. It was a modest affair. We went to the

cinema, then out for a meal in a local restaurant. For the moment, though, we had to rein ourselves in as we still had to save up for a deposit. If I was going to become respectable, things would have to be different. There'd be no more long holidays driving around Spain on the understanding that Steve would bung me an extra wedge if I needed it. In a life on the edges of crime there had been no worries about money.

But now that I had a job with prospects, Vittoria and I could make another step forward. I was to be introduced to her parents. She would take me down to see them on one of her regular Sunday jaunts. As a naturalised Brit, it seems that her father had become more English than the English and Sunday lunch in her childhood home was a sacred institution.

Her parents lived in Kingswood, which was, as it happens, only three miles down the Brighton Road from Banstead. Their house was in a private estate off a long drive. Each of the mansions there was surrounded by a large garden. It could not have been more different from Kensal Town.

Rather than dress up for the occasion, I had to dress down. It was only working-class men who wore their best suit on a Sunday. I now wore a suit on weekdays to work in the City. For Sunday lunch, I was to wear cavalry twill slacks, brown brogues and a cashmere jumper. Welcome to the middle classes, ladies and gents.

While I felt like I was doing the right thing, when we

arrived in Kingswood, I realised this might have been a mistake as Vittoria's father was wearing tweeds. This, I discovered, was part of his attempt to play the role of an old-fashioned English country gentleman. But the fact that I was dressed more casually showed due deference apparently. He was the old dog; I was the young whippersnapper.

Vittoria's mother showed me around the garden, which was very well kept. My mother would have been impressed. Then, in the front room, she offered us all a glass of sherry before lunch. But her father gave me a sly look and suggested instead that the two of us walk across the common to the local pub.

For a moment, I wondered whether this was a slight, ill-disguised reference to my working-class roots. Us plebs get tanked up down the pub before Sunday dinner. Vittoria later explained that it was not such a thing. He just wanted to get me on my own to size me up, while leaving Vittoria and her mum together to swap their own impressions.

It was a sunny Sunday and cricketers in their whites were making an early start on the village green. On our way to the pub, we talked about my new job. Vittoria's father was rather impressed that I had landed a position with such a prestigious firm. I didn't let on what a junior post I held, nor how pitiful the salary was. But clearly he knew his way around the City, in his line of business, dealing with banks and brokers there, so probably he had a clear idea of the situation. I guess even so my job was respectable and had prospects. If he had known my links to crime, I doubt that I would've made it across his threshold.

In the saloon bar of his local, the talk was of the hold-up of a security van in nearby Banstead. This brought me up short, given I knew the whole story from the other side. Some of the locals were amazed at how audacious the robbers had been. Others were worried about what the world was coming to. Armed robberies were things that happened up in London, not here, out in the countryside.

A couple of people complained that they were inconvenienced by the traffic hold-up the robbery had caused, almost proudly claiming some spurious notoriety for having been witnesses to the incident. I wondered how they would have coped if they had actually come up against Mickey wielding a sawn-off.

As it was, I found it difficult to join the conversation. All I could do was nod my head at appropriate junctures and mutter agreement with the general sentiment. I could hardly offer any insight or volunteer the facts as I knew them. When Vittoria asked me later how the trip to the pub with her father had been, I could only be vague and non-committal as the pub conversations had spooked me. She knew nothing of the family's involvement in the hold-up. Nor did I want her to

know. But it worried me that I was intending to marry someone whom I was always going to have to keep secrets from. It
was hardly a basis for a happy married life, for a middle-class
woman at least. Working-class women like my mother knew
not to ask and preferred being kept in the dark. That way they
could cherish illusions about their men and would not have to
make up lies if they were questioned by the police.

If I married a girl from my own class, she would not
expect to know what me or my family got up to, especially if
it was a bit shady. They would understand, it would go without saying. But in the middle classes, it seemed, spouses were
supposed to share.

Thankfully, Sunday lunch passed off without incident.
We talked about cricket and the state of the nation. I took
little interest in politics so it was not difficult to agree with
everything Vittoria's parents said. As we took our leave in the
late afternoon, after tea, I got the impression that they
thought I was a 'sound chap'. On the drive back to town, Vittoria told me that her mother had said that I was quite a
catch. Little did she know that what Vittoria had really
caught was a family that had brought robbery and mayhem
to their very doorstep.

The matter of her older brother came up. Why had he not
been there for Sunday lunch, I asked. Then she broke it to me.
Alexander had been on duty. He was a detective in the Met.

That was a bit awkward as I had shared my family's distrust of the police over apple crumble.

Her brother being in the Met shouldn't have troubled me too much as, in those days, most coppers seemed to be bent. Also, as I was determined to stay away from a life of crime, even if he was straight, I didn't see that having a cozzer in the family was going to present a serious problem.

Nevertheless, I knew enough to put Steve and Mick – not to mention myself – away for a long time. It was all too close for comfort. And what would happen if another hard man in the gang knew that I was dating, or even married to, the sister of a cop?

# CHAPTER NINE
## A DEN OF THIEVES

I had taken a job in the City to get away from a life of crime. What I found was that I had walked into a den of thieves. The City was awash with dodgy money from around the world. No one much cared where it came from, nor where it was going to – as long as our firm got its cut.

As far as I could make out, the money came from the Middle East where backhanders from oil companies had to be quietly disposed of without the authorities knowing about it. There was cash from arms deals and money from dodgy dictators, ripping off impoverished Third World countries to build up a nice nest egg for when they were forced into an early retirement by the next bunch of revolutionaries. There was, of course, drugs money to launder and, with the fall of the Berlin Wall, cash from the Eastern European criminals who were asset-stripping the old centralised communist states. Then with the collapse of the Soviet Union came the biggest prize of all – Russian money. The oligarchs and other bandits chose the City of London as the first port of call for their money. The City was, like me, respectable and above reproach, just as long as you didn't look too closely or ask too many questions.

British banks turned a blind eye while City accountants set up shell companies to funnel the money through Jersey, the Isle of Man, Gibraltar, the Cayman Islands, Panama, Luxembourg, Liechtenstein, Switzerland, anywhere where the authorities were suitably compliant. Someone had to direct this torrent of cash and keep count of where the money was going. The last thing thieves want is people thieving from them. All we had to do was hold our noses and close our eyes.

Shell companies and questionable banks in places where the banking regulations were, shall we say, lax, needed auditors to make everything look above board. This was a gift for City accountants. We were, in effect, policing ourselves. And we had professional help. Former members of the Inland Revenue and HM Customs and Excise – when they were separate entities – and the Serious Fraud Office were paid many multiples of their old government salaries to show us what we could get away with. They knew all the dodges. What they didn't know wasn't worth knowing. They were gamekeepers turned poachers. It was the completion of my education. In a couple of months, I learned more than my years at college ever taught me.

While our firm and the others in the City prided ourselves on our ability to skirt the regulations, sometimes things did go wrong. But the general public only got to hear of the worst excesses. However, those cases that have come to light will give you some idea of what we were getting up to, without breaking any confidences.

For example, in the 1980s, the Bank of Credit and Commerce International (BCCI), which had headquarters in London and Karachi as well as offshoots in Geneva, Luxembourg and Grand Cayman, was investigated for money laundering and other financial crimes. Among its customers were Iraqi president Saddam Hussein, the then dictator of Panama and drug smuggler Manuel Noriega, the dictator of Bangladesh Hussain Muhammad Ershad and the president of Liberia Samuel Doe, as well as criminal organisations such as the Medellín Cartel and the terrorist Abu Nidal's Revolutionary Council, which was responsible for killing over 300 people and injuring over 650. Abu Nidal himself was killed in Baghdad in 2002, reportedly on the orders of that other BCCI client Saddam Hussein.

BCCI was also used by the Reagan administration in the Iran-Contra affair, where American government officials secretly organised the sale of arms to Iran in the face of an international embargo to finance the Contra rebels who were seeking to overthrow the left-wing Sandinista government in Nicaragua. Police and financial regulators nicknamed BCCI the 'Bank of Crooks and Criminals International'.

When it was closed down in 1991, the liquidators, Deloitte & Touche, filed a lawsuit against the bank's auditors, Price

Waterhouse and Ernst & Young, which was settled for $175 million. All three companies were, of course, City accountants. When BCCI's books were opened, hundreds of millions of dollars were missing. It turned out that shareholders were taking out massive loans using their own shares as collateral. These turned out to be worthless. Look it up in Wikipedia. I did. Yes, even though it's an international pariah we have the internet in North Cyprus. I also have a fancy dictionary on my MacBook Pro so I apologise for using fancy words.

But BCCI was only the very large tip of a massive iceberg. Companies' assets were overvalued to get massive loans, while profits were minimised to trim dividends and taxes. These practices were widespread. They permeated the whole system. In the Thatcher years especially, even the ordinary punter could get their income inflated on paper to get a mortgage while, simultaneously, have it deflated to avoid income tax. Everyone was at it.

As far as I could see, the takings from these crimes massively outweighed anything you could get by walking into a branch of Barclays with a shotgun. True, the crimes in the City did not risk anyone being shot, not within the City at least, but there were plenty of people in Africa, South America and the former Soviet Union who were losing their lives as a consequence. Even when 'God's banker' Roberto Calvi was killed after the collapse of the Banco Ambrosiano in 1982, his body was found hanging under Blackfriars Bridge, which is outside the City (just).

It seemed I had jumped from the frying pan into the fire. Crime in the City certainly dwarfed anything Steve and Mick got up to. But at least it kept Vittoria and her parents onside. And, as before, I kept schtum. They did not need to know what crimes I was committing in the ledgers and paperwork. As far as they were concerned, I went to work in a suit, with a pen rather than a sawn-off and a briefcase instead of a heavy, lined swag bag.

Meanwhile, for Steve and Mick, armed robbery was going out of fashion. Security vans had been strengthened. Now, you needed an oxyacetylene torch to cut through the body-work and there wasn't time for that. The windows were bulletproofed and the windscreen toughened so you couldn't smash it with a sledgehammer.

Regular firms were persuading their employees to open a bank account so that they could be paid by cheque and, in due course, by bank transfer direct into their account. When cash had to be carried, it was put in cases that, if forced open, would spray dye on to the notes, making them unusable.

Undaunted, Steve and Mick came up with another ruse. It was another variant on bank robbery – breaking into safety deposit boxes. Their target was a bank in Holborn that had a very impressive vault with a huge steel door. Next door to the bank, there was a flower shop. After that there was an old-fashioned tailor's shop with an unused basement. Steve managed to rent it for cash.

Next he donned a suit and a flat cap and visited the bank carrying a furled umbrella. He used this to get a rough measure of how far the vault was from the wall, so they did not risk popping up in the wrong place. He then calculated that they would have to tunnel exactly 52 feet from the tailor's basement, under the flower shop, to emerge under the vault.

The tunnelling took about three weeks as they could only tunnel at the weekends when the bank and the flower shop were closed, otherwise they risked being heard by the people working in the florists or the bank staff. A shift would be sent in on Friday evening and leave on Monday morning. Eight tons of rubble had to be excavated, which was left piled up in the basement.

When they reached the reinforced concrete floor of the vault, they tried drilling through it – with no success. Mick bought a thermal lance, but that was no good either. Eventually, Steve called in an old safe breaker who blasted his way through it with gelignite. Fortunately the concrete floor was not wired to the alarm system, as it was thought to be impenetrable. Not that it would have made much difference. There are not many people about in Holborn in the small hours. Besides, as we have since learned from the raid on the diamond depository not half a mile away in Hatton Garden in 2015, people take precious little notice of alarms going off if they can't see anything happening above ground.

Nevertheless, fearing the explosion may have been heard, the boys panicked and did not take the time to examine the stash. All they could do was grab a bunch of the boxes and make a run for it. A van was waiting outside. The boxes were loaded into it and taken to a garage Steve had rented, where they could be opened at leisure.

There was a good haul of expensive jewellery and cash, which I imagine the owner was keeping safe from the taxman. They should have worked in the City. Then there was some kiddy porn that could be used against the owner of the box, if they could be identified. On top of that, there were a couple of dodgy guns and some compromising letters and photographs. These, presumably, were being kept safe for blackmail purposes, so they were immediately put to use.

As the owners of much of the contents of the safety deposit boxes could hardly own up to it, the heist did not get much play in the media. The Hatton Garden heist only hit the headlines because legitimate gem dealers kept their stock in there overnight. And without high-powered people complaining about the loss of their valuables, the police didn't have much of an incentive to do anything about it.

It seemed, once again, that my brothers and their friends

were not the only criminals in town – nor, judging from the contents of some of the boxes, the worst. The whole world seemed to be up to something dodgy. But I was still determined to keep myself clean for the sake of Vittoria. Admittedly, I was doing dodgy stuff too at work, but that was for the firm and their clients, not for myself. I still yearned for a respectable marriage, children and a quiet life in the suburbs. I wanted nothing to do with the proceeds of crime. Shame that's not the way it would turn out.

# CHAPTER TEN
## DEAL WITH THE DEVIL

Mum was still talking about moving to Bexhill. Dad was not so keen. He wanted to stay with his mates in the area. It was not a good choice. Despite spending much of his adult life in jail, the old boy thought he should have one more go.

Borrowing a couple of shooters from Mick, he and Uncle Jack went back into the post office business. They avoided main branches as they were too well defended, blagging smaller post offices instead, though the takings were less. They got away with a couple. But one brave postmaster, spotting that the two masked gunmen coming into his shop were rather decrepit, took them on. He grabbed Dad's shotgun. In the tussle it went off, blasting a hole in the ceiling.

The postmaster's wife, who was in the back room, called the cops while Dad and Uncle Jack scarpered. Practically old-aged pensioners, they were not quick on their feet. And it was not like they had gone into training for the heist. The postmaster gave chase. As Dad fiddled to get the key in the ignition of his car, the postmaster took down the registration number. They hadn't even taken the simple precaution of nicking a car for the job.

The Flying Squad were quickly on them. They spotted the car while Dad was driving home. Knowing that Dad and Uncle Jack were armed, they loosed off a couple of shots and blew the tyres out. Claiming that they were in fear of their lives from two armed desperados, the police started spraying bullets around. One hit Dad, wounding him in the stomach. He was taken to hospital where he was stitched up. He recovered, though his health permanently suffered. Stopping a bullet was hardly going to improve your condition, particularly when you are almost an OAP. Uncle Jack came off unscathed, except for the handcuffs.

On reflection, I don't think it was a good idea for Steve and Mick to turn up in court. It didn't help Dad's case to be seen with two other known criminals. The police were pleased to see them there though. They had long wanted to get their cuffs on the boys again, and now they had reason to focus on it. Sticking up for Dad and Uncle Jack confirmed the suspicions in the Plod's minds that we were a crime family that belonged behind bars.

The media had a good time too. Steve and Mick had always tried to stay out of the press. But here they were in their silk suits in a courtroom, showing their support for a couple of aged armed robbers. Libel laws meant that the papers couldn't come right out and accuse Steve and Mick of being armed robbers themselves, but they certainly implied it.

Heavily. This convinced them once and for all to stay out of the limelight and stay out of the media.

I am not sure that it was a good idea for me to turn up in court either. It probably would've been best not to be seen with my brothers and tarred with the same brush. Vittoria was not thrilled either. She had warmed to my dad as a loveable old rogue. Now here he was a dangerous criminal.

I am sure that Vittoria must have had second thoughts at this point. What was she getting herself into? But she was understanding. She loved her dad and thought it only right that I loved my dad too, whatever he had done. And I was harmless, an accountant with a respectable firm in the City, untainted by crime. Or so she thought.

My employer was not so kind-hearted. Despite the dodgy dealings that went on behind closed doors, they were a respectable and respected firm. Like the rest of the City, while sailing close to the wind, they depended on their reputation to do business. They couldn't afford to be seen to have any ties to criminals. I was told that I should consider my position. That was a euphemism. It's City speak for get lost.

I was not making much money. Though I had learned the accountancy business, I was not getting the promotion I'd been promised. I guess I really didn't fit in. The Big Bang had not really taken off yet, so the square mile was not yet packed with young working-class men swigging Dom Pérignon and snorting coke in lap-dancing clubs. Besides, those guys were traders, not lowly paid accountants. The higher-ups in my firm were all public-school boys. Vittoria got on with them well enough at company events, but I was cold-shouldered. I was not 'one of us', as Mrs Thatcher would have said. In other words, I was lonely, looked down on, underpaid and miserable.

Big brother Steve came to the rescue. If I was not happy in the City, he said, I should quit. I knew the accountancy business. It was time for me to set up on my own. He would fund the start-up. And he would line up a lucrative client for me – himself. Indeed, I could handle the financial affairs of the entire Firm.

I had my misgivings. This was the last thing I wanted. I was trying to escape the world of dodgy dealings, both in the City and the underworld of crime. But he then offered me a sweetener. By this point, Dad had pulled another ten years. Despite his age and failing health, he and Uncle Jack were sent back to the Scrubs. Without Dad, Mum was keener than ever to move to Bexhill to be near her friend. Mick had a posh flat in the West End, while Steve himself was shacking up with his girlfriend Maureen. So Vittoria and I could have the house in Portland Road all to ourselves, if we wanted.

For Vittoria, this was the clincher. On my pitiful salary, we had made little progress in saving for a deposit on a semi in the suburbs. She had always loved the house in Notting

Hill with its garden. And she could see the potential. Other houses in the road were being done up. The whole area was on the up and up. The Tube station at Notting Hill Gate was on the Central line, giving a good connection to the West End and the City, not to mention the Circle and District lines if you wanted to go that way. Then there was the station at Ladbroke Grove that was on the Hammersmith & City line as well as the Circle. You could get to all the main overground stations and, with one change, to the airport. Location, location, location, as someone once said.

There was good street parking, now the young vandals were being squeezed out. The houses were large and well built. Prices were rising and we would be sitting on a gold mine. Rather than going on scrimping and saving for years, we could get married and start a family straight away. The house was large enough for us to have as many kids as we wanted.

The only problem was that I was making a deal with the devil and I knew it. But my father and uncle were criminals. My two older brothers were criminals. Now my future wife, whom I had depended on to keep me out of a life of crime, was, unknowingly perhaps, forcing me to get into bed with them. Again, I was in an invidious position. There is little gender equality in the world of organised crime. So how much should a girlfriend, fiancée or wife know? As little as possible for their own protection.

The house had originally been bought with the proceeds of crime. My accountancy practice would be set up using money from the same source. My main client – and as it soon transpired, my only client – was a criminal organisation. And I would be using methods that were barely legal to launder their money. What was I to do? Perhaps a life of crime was my fate. Was there ever anything I could do about it?

# CHAPTER ELEVEN
## THE PROPOSAL

So it was decided. I quit my job and moved into an office in Edgware Road. Steve bought Mum a large apartment with a sea view in Bexhill. I helped her move down there. She wanted to take some of her furniture from Portland Road. The apartment had a large guest room, so I stayed down there for a week while she settled in. There was plenty of shopping to do to get all the things she needed to make herself comfortable, so I wasn't bored.

With Mum on the south coast, I took over visiting Dad in prison. It was a depressing reminder of my childhood. Dad was cheerful enough though. He had spent so many years in jail, he was used to it. It was a home away from home and he was around friends. High in the criminal pecking order (having years under your belt and being an armed robber put you near the top), no one gave him any trouble. Least of all the screws. And, as a veteran of the prison system, he was useful, helping the younger offenders learn the ropes.

Vittoria gave up her flat and moved into Portland Road. I was back on the payroll with Steve, as his accountant, and, with no rent to pay, we had plenty of money to buy new furniture to replace those pieces Mum had taken with her and give the place a makeover. This time it was Vittoria's turn to demonstrate her good taste.

I must admit that it was with some trepidation that I faced the next step. Given Vittoria's parents were reasonably strict Catholics, she hadn't told them that we were living together, though they may have guessed it. The next step, for their sake if not our own, was marriage.

And there was a problem. Although Vittoria had kept my criminal connections – as much as she knew about them – from her parents, they could hardly have failed to notice the coverage of my dad's trial. I knew they liked me, but perhaps only as a boyfriend for their precious daughter, not as a husband. Everyone has seen or read enough about organisations like the Mafia to know the consequences of marrying into a crime family, and I knew that Vittoria would not marry me without her parents' – particularly her father's – approval. She was an old-fashioned girl like that.

The key to this was her older brother Alex. As a copper, he held some sway with her dad. Vittoria consulted him and he gave me the benefit of the doubt. Even though my brothers did, I had no criminal record. I also had severed my ties with the snooker hall, which everyone in Scotland Yard knew was a gangsters' lair. The Serious Fraud Office had some doubts about the dealings of the City accountancy firm I had worked for, especially its connections to various foreign criminals. But I had quit. It appeared, or could be made to appear, like I had done so for ethical reasons. That was another gold star. What he did not know was that now I had set up my own accountancy practice, my only client was Steve and his consortium. But to clear our way to the altar, I had to meet him, win him round and get him on our side.

Thanks to Vittoria, I had been elevated into the middle classes, so we invited him and his girlfriend round for that classic middle-class tradition: a dinner party. They, too, were impressed with the house. He mentioned what a dodgy reputation this area had had, but he could see for himself how things were changing.

The following weekend, Vittoria went down to see her parents on her own. It seemed that our stratagem had worked. Her brother liked me and assured them that there was not a stain on my character. You are, of course, innocent until proven guilty. In fact, I got brownie points for emerging from my background without a criminal record. I was Mr Clean.

The next thing to do was to invite my prospective in-laws to the house. Having convinced them that, as an accountant, I was respectable, they had to see the house so that they would know that I could keep their daughter well looked after.

They, too, knew of the reputation of the area, but when they saw the house and how the neighbourhood was changing they were impressed. Vittoria's mum was particularly taken with the garden and promised to give Vittoria some cuttings.

Meanwhile, I didn't return the compliment that her father had paid me when I had visited and didn't take him to the pub. The patrons in Notting Hill might also be discussing a local crime, but from a very different perspective. Instead he joined me for a glass of whisky in the room Vittoria had kitted out as my study. She had given it an oldie-worldie feel that I thought he would enjoy.

He was concerned that I had quit my job in the City but, as a businessman in his own right, he did not disapprove of me setting up on my own. I told him that I already had one important client. It promised to be a very lucrative account. And I had contacts. Others in the same business were interested in my services. I was, perhaps, over-egging the pudding here, but everyone needs an accountant, if only to keep the Inland Revenue off your back. Look what happened to Al Capone.

Vittoria's father was an old-fashioned man, so I paid him the compliment of doing what I had read about in books. I asked him for his daughter's hand in marriage. When I asked, he didn't jump at it. Rather, he thought about it for a moment. This could've been for show, but I'm pretty sure it wasn't. I imagine that, given the value of his house in Surrey, he followed property prices. I noticed that he had the *FT* in his sitting room at home. Marriage would give her a half-share in a large house in an up-and-coming area in central London, so he could be certain that his daughter would want for nothing. However, he said, I should also ask her mother.

Over beef Wellington, which Vittoria had cooked in her father's honour (Wellington is still much respected in Spain as the victor in the Peninsular War, she tells me), I told her mum that Vittoria and I had discussed marriage and I had already asked her husband's permission. Now I needed her blessing.

She had already looked around the house and, from our domestic arrangements, it was clear that we were living together. So, graciously, she demurred. Vittoria's father then raised a toast to the grandchildren we were going to give them. Sons, he hoped. Vittoria and her mum sucked their teeth. Then they began to discuss which room would make the best nursery.

That night, after they'd left, I went down on one knee and presented Vittoria with a diamond ring, bought with money that Steve had subbed me. (At least he didn't steal one for me.) I'd read enough old-fashioned novels to know how these things were done properly and felt like this was the done thing. But, as I said before, this is not a love story, so I will leave that mushy stuff there.

Steve and Mick were surprised but not shocked by the news. They kinda knew it was coming, but didn't expect it to happen so fast. I had largely kept them away from Vittoria as I really didn't want her involved in any way with that side of my family. I wanted the two parts of my life to be kept entirely separate. Or, at least, this was my intention. Some hope.

Mick felt that I was leaving the family, cutting myself off from them with my posh fiancée. Steve knew better. With shares in the accountancy firm, the house, the ring, he knew he had his hooks into me and that I wasn't going anywhere.

# CHAPTER TWELVE
## THE WEDDING

I had enough to do setting up my new business without bothering about the wedding arrangements. Besides, in the old-fashioned way, these things were supposed to be handled by the bride's family. Vittoria and her mum would make the arrangements. Her father would pay. Meanwhile, after going through the scant documents Steve gave me concerning The Firm's financial arrangements, all I had to do was organise the stag do and order the whistles and flutes (suits) for the groom's party. That is, Steve, Mick, Terry and Curtis, who was going to be best man. I told Steve I was heading over to Moss Bros to hire them, but he forbade it. He handed over a wodge of money. You never know when you might need a morning suit again, he said. Did he think I was going to be invited to Buckingham Palace, or Ascot?

I don't know why I consented to it, but the stag do, it was decided, would be in Amsterdam. Steve and Mick had some contacts in Holland who would make sure we had a good time. Let's draw a veil over it right there.

Vittoria was a Catholic and it was important to her to be married in a Catholic church. I was not particularly religious, but it is possible for a Catholic to marry a non-Catholic in a Catholic church. Vittoria's dad checked with the bishop. We did so on the understanding that any children would be brought up as Catholics. I had no objections to that.

The reception was held back at her parents' place. The house alone was big enough, but they had a marquee erected in the garden. It was a sunny day and Mum had a wonderful time, listening intently to the gardening tips volunteered by Vittoria's mum. I could hardly have refused an invitation to Steve and Mick. They promised to be on their best behaviour. Steve was, of course. He loved playing the gentleman. He turned on the charm and even toned down the bling for the occasion, while Mick tried to cop off with a bridesmaid.

I thought it might be a little awkward having Steve and Mick there, with Vittoria's policeman brother walking around. But in fact, they got on quite well. Steve particularly really clicked with him. Clearly they knew some of the same characters. They also appeared to be probing each other to see what else each other knew. It made me wonder whether, perhaps, Vittoria's brother had given the green light to the marriage so that he would have a fresh source of intel for his bosses.

The honeymoon was to be in Acapulco. Again Steve paid. I can see now that that and the stag do in Amsterdam were all part of a more sinister plan, as these destinations would play an important part in The Firm's future dealings. But, at the time, it just seemed the perfect destination, not least so I could practise my Spanish. Vittoria and I were beginning to speak Spanish at home as we planned to bring up our children to be bilingual.

Vittoria was also keen on Acapulco. There were more of her family in Mexico. They had moved there after the death of General Franco; the hard-line regime in Mexico was more to their taste than the liberal administration that had taken over back home in Spain. They also did business to the south in Central America, including the banks in Panama that I had used to shelter offshore accounts when I had worked in the City. Her cousins there would make useful contacts. So my honeymoon turned out to be more of a business trip.

# CHAPTER THIRTEEN
## THE BUSINESS

When we returned home, it was time for me to get down to business. I had to come up with a set of books that made the snooker hall look like a regular business, with Steve, Mick and me as directors and a few other close associates as employees. Then I had to register the business with Companies House, file annual reports and tax declarations, minimising what was owed, of course. That's what I had been trained to do. The Inland Revenue and Customs and Excise – we were handling booze and were VAT registered – would be keeping their eye out for anything untoward, so everything had to appear above board.

The next problem was that there were stacks of cash around the place that had come from various criminal enterprises. Some of it was still buried in the back garden. This could not be accounted for or go through bank accounts in the normal way. It had to be laundered.

There are many ways to do this. With relatively small amounts, you can do this by betting. With larger amounts, you split it up into smaller sums. This is called smurfing. Then find yourself a bet and put money on every possible outcome.

You could go to a casino, play roulette and bet on both red and black. One will win, the other will lose, unless the ball lands on zero. Otherwise you walk away with the same amount you started with. When you cash in your chips, there will be a record that the money you are walking out with is your winnings and, consequently, legit.

Of course, if you do that in a casino, it is pretty obvious that something dodgy is going on, but you could make a tour of betting shops and back every horse in the race. When you collect your winnings, the only thing you have lost is the vig – that's short for vigorish, which is effectively the fee the bookie takes on the bet. You keep a record of your winnings and forget about your losses. Most gamblers do that anyway. But as far as anyone investigating is concerned, you got the cash legitimately by betting.

It works so much better if you buy a betting shop. That way you keep the vig too. Buying any business that handles a lot of cash is useful. Your dodgy dough can be laundered alongside the legitimate cash that is coming through the business. Pubs, clubs, strip joints, market stalls, all these are good – not brothels, though, as they have their own problems. But the best business to get into was the bureaux de change, and there were plenty around our area because of tourists flocking to Portobello Road antiques market carrying foreign currency with them.

The highest denomination UK note is £50. The euro has a €500 note. Back in the day, the Dutch had a 5,000-guilder note, which was worth around £1,400. So it was easy to change large amounts of sterling into a slim wad of foreign cash that you could slip into your pocket, or a wallet or handbag, when you were travelling abroad and no one would be any the wiser.

We used to use a small bureau de change in Notting Hill where we would take bags of notes that were sometimes contaminated with security dye or traces of cocaine, heroin or speed. The courier then came out with a pocketful of high-value foreign currency and head for the airport. One of our guys was well known as KLM's best customer. He made 158 return trips to Holland, often going back and forth every day. Mostly, he wouldn't even leave Schiphol Airport, having handed it on to the next courier in the chain, who would take it to a bank in the Netherlands or Belgium. Then it would be wired to bank accounts in Switzerland or Dubai. From there, it could be used to buy guns or drugs, or even legitimate businesses. If money was needed back in the UK, money could be sent to invest in a business here or just be taken as a loan. If these deals were suitably 'layered' – that is, passed from account to account, or business to business until the origin was untraceable – the authorities wouldn't take the time and effort to unscramble the whole process. The problem was that you couldn't write any of this down. Fortunately, I had a head for figures and could keep all the complex transactions stored in the back of my mind.

The dodgy cash originally taken in could then be shuffled, broken up and used to buy foreign currency from other bureaux de change or branches of Thomas Cook. And if you needed to, the odd note marked with security dye could be cleaned, as I'll explain later.

While I was away on honeymoon, Mick had been a silly boy. He got such a buzz from doing security vans he began to blag them on spec. When he saw a chance, he seized it – with no thought and no planning, and without even telling Steve.

One summer's day, Mick and a couple of mates were having a drink outside a pub in Hendon when a security van came by and stopped outside the supermarket across the road. Blaggers kept their eyes out for things like this. They may not be planning a job, but intelligence was all important in the armed robbery game. Just knowing a security van's stops and schedules may come in useful in future. Any sighting was noted.

The first thing Mick noticed that day was that the guard's security checks seemed a little lax. He appeared distracted and not looking around at his surroundings as he should have been. Mick turned to his mates. This was surely too good an opportunity to miss. They were up for it.

They quickly downed their drinks and stuffed the glasses into a duffle bag one of them was carrying. Just in case someone had noticed them drinking outside the pub before the security van was turned over, they didn't want to leave any fingerprints or DNA behind. They knew the dangers.

A couple of years earlier, two armed robbers had hit a security van in Camden. They got away with £50,000 but, cornered, they had to ditch the getaway car and leg it. As the police scoured the area, the robbers ducked into a pub for a pint until the hue and cry had died down. Unfortunately for the two robbers, the landlord was an ex-cop. He heard the sirens and noticed the two sweaty men in the bar looking furtively at the door. When they had gone, he took the pint glasses they'd been drinking from and gave them to the police. Their fingerprints on the glasses led them to the robbers, who got thirteen years apiece.

In another case that was doing the rounds, an armed robber had shouted at a security guard and was convicted by the DNA in a speck of spit that had landed on the guard's visor. You couldn't be too careful.

Even Mick was not crazy enough to ride around tooled up all the time, but one of his mates had a small flick knife, which right then would have to do. Mick and the other guy put their hands in a bag with their fingers pointing like the barrel of a gun. All three were wearing bandanas and baseball caps which would come in useful on an occasion like this one. The bandana pulled up over the face and the peak of the baseball cap pulled down over the eyes made an effective disguise.

They watched as the guard went into the supermarket with a cash box. There was no point in stopping him then. The cash box would be empty on the way in. They needed to grab him as he was coming out when it would be full.

As the guard came out, two of them confronted him. Pointing his fingers in the guard's face, Mick said, 'Drop the box or I'll blow your fucking head off.'

The man was shocked, surprised. Was this some kind of a joke? Then Mick's other mate came up behind the guard and put his arm tight around his neck, brandishing the knife. Terrified, the guard let out a yell and took a swing at Mick with the cash box.

The other guard in the back of the van saw what was happening and hit the alarm. There was a loud wail and the automated voice blared out: 'THIS VAN IS UNDER ATTACK. PLEASE CALL THE POLICE.'

It was the turn of the robbers to be surprised. Mick's mate holding the guard loosened his grip. The guard managed to wriggle free and legged it, carrying the cash box and pursued by the three would-be robbers.

Panicking, the guard ran down the street and into the first open door. It was a newsagent's shop. He slammed the door shut and leaned on it so the robbers couldn't get in.

Seeing what was going on, the other customers started scream-ing and tried to get out the back.

The guard struggled to hold back Mick and his mates, who were hell-bent on getting the cash, while passers-by stopped to watch the fracas and the security guard in the van called the police.

The robbers only had moments to spare, but Mick was not about to give up. He sat down on his arse on the pavement and began kicking at the bottom panel of the door until it splintered. The guard then abandoned the door and fled to the back of the shop and hid behind the counter.

The three robbers were now in the shop. Still brandishing his make-believe gun, Mick yelled, 'Throw the fucking box out or get shot.'

With nowhere else to go, the guard took what he judged to be the sensible option. He chucked the box out, which slid across the floor to the robbers' feet. Mick grabbed the box and the three robbers fled.

They quickly split up, with Mick hanging on to the cash box. Sirens were approaching, so he dashed down a side street. There was no way he could make it back to his car which he had left, thoughtlessly, in the pub car park.

As he rounded a corner, he saw an old lady getting out of a black cab. He was inside before she had paid the fare. The taxi took him to Steve's place. Steve was not at home, but his girlfriend Maureen let Mick in. He told her to phone Steve while he set about breaking into the cash box. Some of them had a GPS tracking device, so time was of the essence.

He levered the padlock off with a large screwdriver, but then heard the telltale pop and buzz of a dye pack going off. This essentially rendered the cash useless. Dyed notes could hardly be handed in at the bank. They were easy to spot and most retailers would report them straight away, knowing they had come from a robbery.

You could get the dye off by soaking the notes in a bathtub of white spirit and biological washing powder for forty-eight hours. Then you had to fish out each banknote and hang it up to dry, before ironing each one individually. One team found an easy way round this. They sorted out the notes that were only slightly dyed along the edges, then went out to a busy street and chucked half the haul in the air. The crowd went mad grabbing the cash as it came fluttering down. The robbers were now covered. If they got caught trying to pass dyed notes, they would not be the only ones. Everyone in the area had some.

For Mick, though, cleaning the notes wouldn't be an option. As soon as the lid sprung open, red smoke billowed out, filling the room. This instantly marked everything it touched. Mick flung the window open to let out the smoke, coughing like he was a hundred-a-day fag smoker.

Maureen had the sense to slam the living room door, but

yelled for Mick to get out of her house and take his stupidness with him. Mick emerged red-faced and literally red from head to toe. He stuffed £20,000 of dyed notes into a holdall and wrapped the cash box, which was still smoking, in double-layered bin bags.

'You'd better get rid of everything from the living room,' he told Maureen.

Steve was not best pleased when he got home. There would need to be new curtains, carpets and furniture to pay for, and the whole place would have to be cleaned and repainted. But first the two of them went off to dump the smoking cash box in a bin somewhere distant. Mick had to burn his clothes and stay indoors for a couple of weeks, showering frequently, until the dye wore off.

Then Mick called his mates to divvy up. Steve took £2,000 off the top, though he had not been in on the raid. Some £3,000 were singed or dyed beyond use and were chucked out of the window of his car in the high street. That left Mick and the boys £5,000 each, which they would have to pass on on a dark night. Otherwise, they would have to buckle down and do another sort of money laundering than the type I was used to.

For the money, this felt like a stupid move. No one got hurt and they were not even carrying guns, but the police would not have seen it that way if they'd got caught. Amateur robbers figured that if they used an unloaded gun or an imitation firearm in an armed robbery, they would be treated lightly by the courts. That's not the case. In robbery, it's the threat that counts. Whether you're carrying a Dirty Harry-style Smith & Wesson Model 29 .44 Magnum loaded with hollow-point dumdum bullets or a potato carved into the shape of a pistol, if the victim is genuinely in fear of their life, the effect is the same and you are going away for a long stretch.

In the late 1980s, there was an East End stick-up merchant the tabloids called 'Cucumber Man'. He robbed a number of building societies with a cucumber in a paper bag. It was said that he ate the cucumber in a sandwich afterwards. He got nine years.

Later, a young lad from Woolwich used a banana and got away with several thousand. He too was said to have eaten it afterwards. He went down for ten years.

Then there was an idiot who put a Cornflakes packet with wires coming out of it on the counter in a building society and passed a note to the cashier saying it was a bomb. He was going to blow the place up unless they handed over the cash. Surprisingly, this worked for a few blags. Eventually the building societies twigged and he was caught. Seven years.

Again, Steve was not well pleased with Mick. An ad hoc raid like that threatened the whole operation. He decided they had to get more serious.

# CHAPTER FOURTEEN
## THE FOOTSTEPS OF GIANTS

When it happened in 1963, the Great Train Robbery was the biggest robbery in UK history. The blaggers had got away with £2.6 million, which would be worth £70 million now. The robbery was audacious and meticulously planned. They would have got away with it if there hadn't been a slip-up over the cleaning of the farmhouse they used as a headquarters.

The robbers stopped a night mail train travelling from Glasgow to London. One of the carriages was an HVP (high-value packages) coach. It was carrying packages containing cash from the banks in Scotland. Normally, the haul would be worth £300,000, but there had been a bank holiday north of the border where everyone had been spending freely, so they were in for a bumper payday.

The robbers didn't carry guns, but when they boarded the train, the train driver Jack Mills took on one of the gang and was struck over the head. The HVP coach was then detached and ransacked. Within thirty minutes, the robbers had made off with the loot.

Despite the injury to Mills, who never fully recovered, the robbers were seen as heroes. Though not exactly Robin Hoods, they were working-class lads who had made a blow against the Establishment. It even damaged the standing of the government at the time. The Conservative Party, which had been in power for twelve years, had already been rocked by the Profumo scandal when the British war minister got caught sharing a mistress with the Soviet naval attaché and lied about it to the House of Commons. In the face of such an audacious robbery, the government appeared incompetent. The prime minister resigned and the seemingly young vigorous Labour Party came to power the following year. Meanwhile, there were public protests at the length of the sentences the train robbers got. When Ronnie Biggs and others escaped from prison, people cheered them on and movies were made about them and the robbery itself.

What's more, some of the gang got away. Most of the cash was never recovered and there was talk of a Mr Big who was living somewhere exotic off the bulk of the proceeds.

But the game-changer for our generation was the Brink's-Mat robbery in 1983. These lads had got away with £26 million, which dwarfed the Great Train Robbery even when adjusted for inflation. The robbers targeted a warehouse near Heathrow Airport owned by the Anglo-American security company Brink's-Mat. They had planned to steal around £1 million worth of Spanish pesetas – the currency in Spain before the euro was introduced in 1999. Instead, they found

6,800 gold bars being stored there overnight ready to be shipped to Hong Kong the next day, along with some platinum, $250,000 in travellers' cheques and £100,000 worth of cut and uncut diamonds.

One of the security guards named Tony Black told his brother-in-law, a guy named Brian Robinson, that a 'f***in' huge' amount was going to be stored in the warehouse that night, though even he only thought the haul would be £3 million. Terry Adams, head of the Clerkenwell Crime Syndicate, aka the A-Team, and later jailed for money laundering, put Robinson and his mate Micky McAvoy in touch with a fixer named Brian 'The Milkman' Wright. Together they put together a team to do the job.

They turned up outside the warehouse in a blue Transit van just as it opened at 6.30am. Unlike the Great Train Robbers, they were armed. Tony Black arrived for work late, at 6.40am. Soon after, he said he was going to the toilet. Instead, he went to the front door and let the robbers in.

Brandishing guns and with balaclavas over their faces, they made the security guards lie on the floor. One, who was slow to react, was knocked to the floor, gashing his head on the edge of a table. The guards were handcuffed, their legs were bound with tape and cloth bags were tied over their heads. Meanwhile one of the robbers tuned a radio into the police frequencies.

Black had already identified the two guards who shared the combination to the vault. The robbers poured petrol over them and threatened to set them on fire if they didn't open it. One immediately complied but the other said that the company had recently changed the combination and he could not remember his half. One of the robbers got a knife out and threatened to castrate him. The guard protested that he was doing his best, but after twenty minutes trying, the robbers gave up.

Instead, they started looking in the various drums and boxes that were scattered around the place. They found scrap silver, tarnished platinum and travellers' cheques, but those would be easily traceable. So maybe they weren't so lucky after all.

They went back to work on the security guard who had said he could not remember his half of the combination. Eventually, and thankfully for the robbers, he remembered. The alarm was neutralised and the vault was opened.

Inside, they found a stack of small boxes, bound with metal straps. Inside each of them, they found twelve gold bars. It was a haul beyond their wildest dreams. There were also several hundred thousand pounds in used banknotes, along with more travellers' cheques and a thousand carats of diamonds.

The robbers began to load the gold bars into their rusty old Transit. The bars weighed three and a half tons and so they had to use the warehouse's own forklift. The van sunk on its suspension and it was as much as the engine could do to haul the load out of the gate. But they were away with more than they ever thought possible to get.

Apparently, the bound guards were found by a mechanic who had come to fix one of their vans. He called the police.

Steve soon heard about the heist. As the robbers knew nothing about disposing of the gold, they had to put out a call far and wide in the underworld for help. And this was where their problems began.

The heist soon made the press where it was dubbed 'the crime of the century'. Consequently, the cops were under enormous pressure to find the culprits and the gold. The insurance underwriters at Lloyd's of London immediately offered a reward of £2 million for information that led to the return of the stolen gold, which was already climbing in value on the London metal market because of the theft. Within a week, the value of the haul had already increased by £1,100,000.

As it was, the police had an easy job. The first thing they did was a background check on the security guards and soon discovered that Black's brother-in-law was one Brian Robinson, who was a well-known armed robber. As this was my brothers' game, they knew all about him. So did the Old Bill.

After a prolonged grilling, Black confessed and picked out a photograph of McAvoy and another blagger known to Steve and Mick. The police didn't pick the suspects up immediately, hoping they would lead them to the gold. Robinson and the other guy continued to keep a low profile, but 'Mad Micky' McAvoy moved out of his council house and into a mansion on the borders of Kent with two Rottweilers which he named Brink's and Mat.

Clearly, McAvoy was taking the piss, so the police swooped and took the three of them into custody. They weren't bothered. They all had alibis and stuck to them. Their brief, well known in criminal circles, entered a writ of habeas corpus. Their alibis were overturned and they were promptly charged.

McAvoy and Robinson were convicted of armed robbery and sentenced to twenty-five years. They served sixteen. Black was sentenced to six years, served two and was given a new identity under the witness protection scheme, aka the UK Protected Persons Service.

Meanwhile, two old-time crooks, Kenny Noye and his mate Brian Reader, had convinced McAvoy and Robinson to let them handle the gold. They knew the business. Gold was a favourite commodity used in VAT fraud. This is a simple swindle. No VAT is paid on gold imported from the EU. And there is certainly no VAT on gold smuggled into the country or otherwise illicitly obtained. However, VAT was charged on gold if it was sold in the UK. It was a simple matter to set up a fly-by-night company, register it for VAT, sell the gold and disappear before the VAT collected on the sale had to be paid to Customs and Excise. Gold was perfect for this form of fraud as its high value meant large returns with the minimum of delay. The price was fixed twice a day by the London gold market so the vendor could not be undercut by commercial competitors and, though heavy, gold was at least compact and relatively easy to transport.

The problem with the Brink's-Mat gold was that the ingots had been assayed and stamped. To pull off any scam using gold bars, you first had to remove the identifying marks, but here the metal itself had a built-in identifier. Gold is never 100 per cent pure. The various impurities act like a fingerprint, so assaying would immediately identify the source. After the Brink's-Mat heist, every legitimate trader would be on the lookout for dodgy gold, especially in the quantities Noye and Reader would be trying to shift. To hide the origin of the gold, it would have to be smelted, impurities introduced, then recast.

Kenny got his hands on a smelter. He and Reader were smelting the gold mixed with copper coins in a shed in the garden of Noye's house in Kent when a deep surveillance officer named DC John Fordham came into the grounds to take a look. He was dressed in camouflage and a balaclava. Noye stabbed him ten times. Charged with murder, he claimed he had killed Fordham in self-defence and was found not guilty. Reader was also charged and acquitted.

While they weren't found guilty of murder, they were later convicted of handling gold from the Brink's-Mat robbery and VAT fraud. They were jailed for fourteen and eight years respectively. Two years after he was released, Noye was convicted of murder in a road rage incident and sentenced to life, serving twenty years. Brian Reader was jailed again in 2016 for masterminding the Hatton Garden safe depository job. Sentenced to six years, he served three.

Others were suspected of handling the proceeds of the Brink's-Mat heist. John 'Goldfinger' Palmer admitted melting down gold bars from the robbery in his garden, but denied knowing they were stolen. However, he paid £360,000 to Lloyd's in settlement of a civil action. He was later convicted of timeshare fraud and sentenced to eight years.

It seems that John had friends in high places in the Met and managed to dodge other charges. His luck ran out in 2015 when he died after being shot six times in the chest by a professional hitman. Others involved in the robbery died in mysterious circumstances.

Brian Wright sought refuge in North Cyprus where he used some of the Brink's-Mat money to fund a gang smuggling £500 million worth of cocaine into Britain. He was only caught when he made a visit to Spain. Extradited to the UK, he was convicted of running an international cocaine empire and jailed for thirty years.

The thing was, despite the £2 million reward, very little of the Brink's-Mat gold was ever recovered. Much of it was thought to have been funnelled into the development of London's Docklands, currently home to some of the world's biggest banks. That money is now, to all intents and purposes, clean. Someone clearly got away with it.

Steve followed Brink's-Mat closely. It seemed to him to be an abject lesson of how not to do it. The gang had let greed overtake them. What was the point in stealing that much gold if they had no way of handling it? With that much money at stake, there were bound to be fallings-out. Others, like Kenny Noye, were bound to step in to syphon off the cream. The heist was doomed from the off because of Black's relationship with Robinson. It was a failure of intelligence and planning, both things that Steve prided himself on.

He was much more impressed by the robbery of the Security Express depot in Shoreditch earlier that year, though it netted only £6 million. It appeared the robbers had done their homework perfectly.

As armed robbers like Mick were always on the lookout for security vans, just in case an opportunity presented itself, the robbers had noticed that Security Express delivered cash to banks first thing in the morning, before they opened to the public. Security guards were seen not just delivering notes which were comparatively light, but also heavy sacks of coins which they humped across the pavement.

While the deliveries were early in the morning, the cash would be kept in the secure vault overnight and its lock would be controlled by a timer. When the vault was opened in the morning, it would be easy enough to load up the security vans with notes, but the gang figured the silver would be loaded up in the evening before the vault was locked and then actually sit in the vans overnight.

It was easy enough to discover where the depot was and the initial plan was to break into the compound and rob the vans at night. However, while casing the joint, it was discovered that the security was pretty lax. The CCTV had a blind spot, so it was easy enough to climb over the fence without being spotted on camera. There were bins in the yard that you could hide behind out of sight of the cameras until the opportunity arose.

In the morning, the guard would come out of the main building and walk to a hatch by the main gate, where they would collect a pint of milk, presumably for their tea. When they did that, they propped the door to the depot open, providing any would-be robber with access to the building.

The robbers decided to hit the building on a bank holiday Monday. This meant that cash would have been coming in from retailers over the weekend. Better still, the Ideal Home

Exhibition was being held at Olympia, helpfully providing a bumper haul. The robbers' aim, Steve surmised, was to get enough money to give up crime and buy into a legitimate business, even if it was on the Costa del Crime.

There may have been an insider who provided information to the gang, but the police never determined who it was. Criminals know that it is never difficult to find some disgruntled security guard who would spill the beans on routines, layouts, procedures and who on the staff was likely to give trouble, provided that they were not on the scene at the time of the heist. For months after a successful robbery, a fat envelope would be shoved through their letter box to ensure their silence. Even more easily than this, it is sometimes possible to learn all you need to know overhearing a conversation between two work colleagues in a pub.

The job itself went smoothly enough. The blaggers got inside the depot first thing in the morning and lay in wait for men with the keys and the codes to come. As it was a bank holiday, they would not be coming in until the afternoon as there would be no cash going out to banks that day, so the vault would only have to be opened when money started coming in from the retailers.

Before the robbers could get the security guards to open the vault, there were some heroics. As at Brink's-Mat, a security guard was threatened with petrol and a box of matches, or so the police and the newspapers said. The robbers denied this. It was not a real threat anyway. They already knew that guards were instructed not to resist if their life was in danger.

The blaggers then loaded cash into a Transit that had been painted to look like a Security Express van and took off. This is where it all went wrong. And it was the fault of poor planning, Steve said.

The robbers didn't have a secure gaff to hide the money while they counted it and divvied it up. It seems that someone let them down and, at the last minute, an otherwise innocent party agreed to let the van stay in his garage until the money was counted and distributed. For this they would get a 'drink' – which turned out to be £15,000.

Apparently the Flying Squad got a tip-off that a couple of the team drank in the Albion pub in Dalston. They put the place under surveillance. The stake-out men soon noticed two well-known robbers with ties to the local crime family in the company of a local garage owner. Months later, when a car thought to have been used in the Brink's-Mat heist was found abandoned outside his garage, the police had an excuse to pull the garage owner in and search his house.

The money was long gone, but police noticed that the place had recently been redecorated. Bank statements and other correspondence revealed that his fortunes had suddenly taken a turn for the better. He had just bought two cars and taken a family holiday in Greece.

He admitted that he had done a favour for a friend and let him use the garage at his home. But, in for fear of his life, wouldn't say who it was. He later withdrew his statement and pleaded guilty to robbery. But from their surveillance, the police knew who his associates were and, aided by one of them turning Queen's evidence, it was easy to show that they had had a windfall around the time of the robbery.

Some had fled to Spain to live the good life, where the authorities were loath to send them back. One had to be practically kidnapped there. Another, fearing that the same would happen to him, returned to the UK and pleaded guilty to handling stolen money.

Now, you probably know who some of these people are, but others got away with it, so I am not going to risk grassing any of them up. The key thing here, as far as Steve was concerned, was that some of them did get away with it and almost none of the money was ever recovered. Who said that crime doesn't pay?

Steve figured that he was a better planner than those who had instigated these heists and that, by studying these cases, he could avoid the pitfalls. After all, the guys that had pulled them off had got away with most of the money and, some of them at least, had retained their liberty. The idea was to up the odds in that department in our favour.

# CHAPTER FIFTEEN
## DOING THE BANK OF ENGLAND

The first thing to do to increase the odds in our favour was to sideline Mick. He had his own interests. From the money he had made, he was running a club on Charing Cross Road. I did the books for it. He surrounded himself with other well-known criminals, which called into question his legitimacy. The police must have been keeping an eye on him and his associates who would probably have sold their own grandmothers if there was a drink in it for them.

Mick was also getting dangerously unstable. He was an adrenaline junkie. He got off on the buzz of armed robbery. And Steve was very aware how that turned out with his previous 'freelance' operation. Steve didn't want someone dousing a security guard with petrol and actually setting them on fire. Nor did he want what he saw as the other pitfall in the Security Express heist – the risk of kidnapping charges for holding security guards hostage. So he had an inspired idea – nick off other criminals. Even better, nick off the Bank of England.

Without Mick in the loop until the dye wore off, Steve came to depend on me more and more. He was a bright guy and figured that there must be other places where money was

stored for circulation to the banks. Having spent time working in the City, I should know about it. I didn't, so I had a
chat with Curtis, who knew his way around the financial
system.

While the money in England was issued by the Bank of
England in Threadneedle Street, not much money was actually held there. It was a gold repository, and Steve wasn't
interested in that, given the trouble the Brink's-Mat mob had.

British coins were minted in Wales, while notes were
printed in Debden, Essex. From there, the money was farmed
out to depots around the country run by various banks and
security firms. They then distributed it to banks, who passed
it on to their customers. Used notes that were dirty or damaged were then passed back to these distribution centres, then
back to Debden where they were incinerated. That seemed to
us to be a terrible waste of money.

Steve and I took a little trip up the M11 to Debden to take a
look. The Bank of England's printworks there lay conveniently
next to junction 5, up a long dead-end street that ran through a
trading estate that was home to a Mercedes-Benz showroom.
After three-quarters of a mile, the street ended in the car park of
the printworks. Beyond that were woods and farmland.

The printworks itself was encircled by a double ring of
fences with security cameras. The access road ran alongside
the fence for nearly 400 yards. Then there was a roundabout.

One exit led to the main entrance, the other to the car park, which lay outside the security fence. We could hardly hang about there as we would have been clocked by the security cameras, but from what we could see, the entrance had two gates, a full 50 feet apart. Between them was a security post that checked incoming and outgoing traffic. This was over-looked by a control tower like you might see at an airfield.

To allay suspicion, we pretended to be lost and consulted a map. This was pre-satnav. As we were turning round, we noticed that the staff moving between the building and the car park also had to go through the main gates with a security check along the way. The place seemed impregnable. Even if you got in there, there was no way you'd get out again.

Crossing the double ring of fences undetected was next to impossible. To approach the main gate you'd either have to be in one of the vans used to transport the banknotes, a maintenance crew or a caterer. If you got through the first gate, you'd be stuck between the two. Even if you pulled a shooter, the control tower would not let you through the second gate, or would detain you long enough for the road outside to be packed with cops.

Nor could you just saunter up with a balaclava and a sawn-off. You'd never even get through the first gate. With the gun concealed and your face uncovered, you might as well chuck away the shooter and walk straight into Wandsworth nick with your hands up. The only way in there was to hire the SAS.

It seemed to me that we were on a fool's errand, but Steve did not give up so easily. Short of a boozer where we might pick up some info, there was an Indian restaurant set back from the road directly across from the printworks. It was already early evening, so we stopped in for dinner. After we had ordered, Steve engaged the manager in conversation. He remarked that it was rather an odd place to have a restaurant. It was at the far end of a trading estate which would have shut up shop early. There was no passing trade. It was not on the main drag and it was quite a way from the high street in Debden, the Broadway, where all the other restaurants were. They must do particularly good curry for people to seek them out, Steve said.

The manager was flattered, but he pointed out the print-works which, he told us with a smile, belonged to the Bank of England. But the employees were civil servants, I said, who usually were poorly paid. No, said the manager, they have money to burn.

Steve and I looked at each other. The manager laughed. Besides printing new money, the manager said, the Bank of England had an incinerator where they burned the old notes. We laughed too, joining in the hilarity.

While we were there, a party of diners came in. They were loud. The guy who had put himself at the head of the table was egging the rest of them on. Having clearly assumed the role of host, he was urging others to order, saying that they were not to worry. He was going to pay for everything.

We lingered over dinner. When we left, we noticed a Merc parked outside the restaurant. Steve took down its registration number. Coming out of the restaurant's car park, we took a wrong turning and drove up to the printwork's car park to take another quick shufti. While most of the cars were modest Fords, Vauxhalls, Volkswagens and the like, there were also a couple of high-end cars – Porsches and BMWs. Turning back past the Indian restaurant, we noticed that the Merc was leaving and there were no other cars in the restaurant's car park. It must've been carrying our fellow diners.

As we drove back down the street towards the main road, Steve noticed that it curved so you were quickly out of sight of the CCTV cameras that ringed the printworks. Either side of the road were the low flat buildings of the trading estate. Steve wanted to check them out and turned off down one of the side streets. It was quiet. All the buildings were closed and no one was around. Emerging back on to the access road from another of the side streets, we had to stop to allow a convoy of security vans heading towards the printworks to pass.

Over the next few days, it was clear that Steve was planning something big. He sent men back to Debden to look around the banks, building societies, travel agents, builders and builders' merchants in the area. They were all doing well.

The team also noted down the registration numbers of flash cars heading to and from the printworks. This could be done easily from the car park of the Debden Sports Club which lay on the main road opposite the street that led to the printworks. The club was only open at the weekend so nobody noticed guys sitting in its car park noting down details of the traffic going in and out of the access road. I took a couple of shifts on the stakeout.

Steve had spent his time analysing what had gone wrong with the previous high-profile robberies. First, you needed a close-knit team that did not depend on any outsiders. That was no problem as we already had the team that had been used in the security van heists who had proved reliable. We wouldn't be using outside contractors like Noye or Reader, or the guy who let the Security Express robbers use his garage.

The Brink's-Mat heist was given away because the security guard Black knew Robinson, the armed robber, but none of us knew anyone in Debden. It was nowhere near our patch. And the other trick in a big heist was that no one should suddenly become wealthy. That was a dead giveaway that the cops could not fail to spot. This was my department.

Before the job Steve was planning, I would restructure our growing empire of businesses – pubs, clubs, car dealerships, pawnbrokers, betting shops, casinos and bureaux de change. While we maintained a controlling interest, each member of the team would be given a share, with a job in management, a fancy title and generous salary, though they wouldn't be expected to do much work. I knew they wouldn't fancy that.

Once the proceeds of the heist were laundered, they would be invested in the various businesses. Then the team members could get their cut by selling their shares or taking their money as a dividend or bonus. That way, the money they got would look kosher.

I didn't know the details of Steve's plan at that point, but it was clear that it centred on the Bank of England's printworks. When it came to getting money out of the country, it was perfectly positioned. Within three miles, the M11 connected to the M25. That in turn connected to the M20 that took you to Folkestone and Dover. Otherwise, you could take the A12/120 direct to Harwich, where ferries sailed for Holland, and Steve had connections in Amsterdam. From there, the money could be sent anywhere in the world.

Steve fancied Spain as he had spent time there. This was not a good idea. While the Spanish took it easy on extraditing British criminals back to the UK, they were part of Europol and did cooperate with the British police when it came to examining bank accounts and business records. I favoured Panama as I had had dealings there before, but I won't go too much into the details as we still do business there now.

Meanwhile, Steve and I pored over maps in his office.

Maureen was not best pleased as she was pregnant with their first child at the time and thought he should be at home looking after her. But he assured her that it was going to be worth it.

Soon we had a complete log of the traffic in and out of the access road and noticed that the security vans came in late in the evening and then – after, presumably, unloading their old notes and picking up new ones – headed out early in the morning. They seemed to be scheduled to avoid times where shifts in the printworks were changing and the road was full of the staff coming and going.

It was the vans going in that we were interested in. They were carrying old notes, which would be untraceable, while the freshly printed ones coming out would have serial numbers that had been noted. But we needed to know more.

Putting together all the intelligence we'd gathered, Steve figured out what was going on. There were the fancy cars in the staff car park and the key businesses in the town that were doing much better than you would expect in the wilds of Essex. The employees of the printworks were way ahead of us. They were pilfering cash. Not the new notes fresh off the press, but old ones that were supposed to be burned up in the incinerator. If some of them had disappeared before they were due to be turned to ashes, who would be any the wiser?

As a scam, it was easy to pull off. You didn't need shooters, masks, getaway cars or the like. Say there were a bunch of you working a shift, pretty soon you'd get to be mates. You'd know you could trust each other. If someone didn't want in on the action, it would be easy enough to pay them to look the other way. They could get their cut outside the building.

The employees walked in and out of the printworks every day. They had ID and the guards on the gate knew them. All they had to do was grab a handful of used notes at the end of their shift and stuff them into their underwear. In fact, the guards probably didn't check the staff's wallets or handbags either. And even if they did, the stolen notes looked like any other. As they were old notes, no one would've made a note of their serial numbers.

If someone got suspicious or there was a change of personnel and it got hot, you could quit for a time – and start again when it was safe. But if you were taking just five £20s a shift, five days a week, fifty weeks a year, that would bring you in £25,000 a year on top of your salary. A nice little bonus. With your everyday expenses already covered by your wages, that would let you buy a nice car, take the family on a nice holiday, go out for a couple of nice meals and give your house a lick of paint, double glazing, an extension and a garden with a water feature.

Steve had a list of the registration numbers of the flash cars we'd seen going to and from the printworks. He had contacts inside the Met who could provide the names and addresses of the owners. I don't want to venture into the realms of conspiracy theories here, but around this time Steve had become a Freemason and on the first Monday or Tuesday of each month would go off to a secretive lodge meeting in the City, in a proper Masonic suit with a black jacket and striped trousers and carrying a black briefcase with his regalia in it.

It's long been alleged that there was a nod and a wink between the Masons and the criminal justice system. *The Times*, *The Sunday Times*, the *Independent* and BBC's *Panorama* programme have all investigated the links between serious organised criminals such as the Adams family and Brink's-Mat gold smelter John Palmer with Scotland Yard via the Masons. The House of Commons Home Affairs Committee even published a report on it, but nothing was done. Just saying. Anyway, Steve seemed to have access to the DVLA's central records.

With the names and addresses of the car owners, Steve would go round and take a look at their gaff. If it was proper posh – mock Tudor with a well-tended garden – it probably belonged to some high-up manager. Someone whose salary matched what they were showing off. What he was looking for was one of Mrs Thatcher's right-to-buy council houses that had been lavished with a little more attention than it deserved.

It was then a case of waiting around until they went to the boozer and getting into a chat with him or her. If they were sunburnt, you'd give them a chance to boast about their holiday. The Maldives? Expensive. Or if you remarked that they were remarkably red in the face, they might say that they worked in hot and sweaty conditions, with an incinerator, say. After a jar or two, you would manoeuvre the conversation around to work and, by closing time, you'd know all you needed to know.

Then it was a job for Mick. Even when he wasn't completely mental, he could still be intimidating. He would pay a visit to one or two of the incinerator staff who seemed to be living above their means. He'd intimate that he knew all about their nice little earner. But their secret was safe. He was a bit of a crook too. All he needed was the rota showing the times big shipments of old notes were coming in. Otherwise, he made it clear, their boss would find out what they were up to.

Armed with the roster, we found a time in the dead of night when two or three security vans were due to come along that half-mile stretch of road towards the printworks that was out of sight of the CCTV cameras. Once the first one was stopped, we could wait until the next ones had backed up behind them, then close off the road.

Our boys knew how to rob a security van. They emerged from the side streets with guns and chainsaws. The operation had also got a little bit more sophisticated over the years. Steve had bought a radio jammer from a shop in Tottenham Court Road. That stopped the guards in the vans contacting security at the printworks or their own company headquarters. As an added precaution, a car was set on fire in Loughton and a 999 call was made to make sure that the cozzers from the nearest police station were busy dealing with that.

Realising quickly that they couldn't summon help, after the first slice of the chainsaw the security guards gave us no trouble. The used cash in the back of the van was not going to be in pouches with dye spray. It was old currency and was going to be burned anyway. In less than three minutes, the team were out of there. Another minute and they were on the M11. By the next morning the money was out of the country.

I'm not telling you how much the haul was, but it was probably the biggest cash robbery at the time, even though many of the notes were in such a poor state they had to be destroyed. Since then there has been the Securitas depot robbery in Tonbridge, Kent, that netted £53 million, taking our crown.

But if it was such a big deal, why haven't you heard about it? That puzzled me too, to start with. There was no mention of it in the media, no splash headlines, no TV news reporters doing a piece to camera in front of the printworks, no outraged calls in Parliament for the criminals to be tracked down – 'jail them and throw away the key' – like there was with the Great Train Robbers. But after a couple of discreet chats with Curtis, I began to figure it out.

I had already learned when I worked in the City that the whole financial system depends on confidence. The Bank of England is a major pillar of the global monetary infrastructure. What would happen if the world and its bankers lost confidence in it? Or in the Federal Reserve?

Capitalism hangs on such thin threads. Some Americans still call the greenback 'script'. It's a promissory note, not money itself. British banknotes still have 'I promise to pay the bearer the sum of . . .' printed on them and are signed by the Chief Cashier of the Bank of England. The printworks at Debden also prints the currency for a dozen different countries around the world. If its security was compromised, it would have a significance in the whole world, not just to the UK.

The raid on the security vans took place in the dead of night in a deserted trading estate in the middle of the Epping Forest. No one saw it. Damaged vans that had been sliced up by chainsaws could easily be towed into the compound of the printworks and be disposed of without anyone outside knowing. So the whole thing could be easily hushed up.

When there was any suspicion that something was up, that was easily remedied. A number of employees were arrested for stealing from the cages where the money due to be incinerated was kept. They are alleged to have stolen £600,000, but as there were no witnesses, only one was prosecuted. He was the lookout who distracted the guards while the others helped themselves. He got only eighteen months.

The group were ordered to pay back £500,000 in a civil suit. The case was eventually dropped by the Bank of England after twenty-six years of litigation. A couple of movies were made about the heist, so the culprits may have benefited there too.

I don't know whether Steve grassed them up to give the police a fall guy and stop them coming after us, but I wouldn't have put it past him. We were now in the big time. Sure, Steve and Mick had dreamt of stealing enough money to quit the world of crime completely. But when is enough enough? Ask any multimillionaire and they will say never. Besides, the money was tied up in front companies so the authorities couldn't claw it back; it's not like having a bulging wad in your pocket when you go out on a Saturday night. There's no slaking the thirst for cash.

Having made a record haul gave us respect among the rest of the criminal fraternity, if not among the general public who did not know about it. It was plain to us that we were never going to top the Bank of England heist, so we were going to have to go into another line of business. And we now had the money to make a serious investment.

# ACT III

## MONEY AND DRUGS

1995–2012

# CHAPTER SIXTEEN
## WORKING FROM HOME

Okay, so we had got away with, at that time, the biggest cash heist in British history, seemingly with Establishment collusion. I can only imagine the Chancellor of the Exchequer going to the Home Secretary asking them to tell Scotland Yard to leave us alone so as not to destabilise the economy. As a sop they could have the insiders who were nicking the handfuls of cash that should have gone into the incinerator. Plod did not pursue the line of enquiry with much vigour, having missed out on the star prize – us. But that did not mean the Flying Squad were not peeved. They were determined to get us for something. The next time we tried anything, they would be on us. So we would have to leave armed robbery out for the moment. We had enough money to be going on with, though. And Steve celebrated by getting married to Maureen. Their first child, a boy, was born soon after.

News of the Bank of England heist had spread through the underworld too. It commanded respect. No one was going to challenge us. Anyone who wanted to do something dodgy on our patch would have to ask permission first then, if successful, give us a substantial cut – or answer to Mickey if the funds were not forthcoming.

On the home front, everything was running smoothly. Vittoria had given up teaching when she was pregnant. She was old-fashioned and wanted to be a stay-at-home mum. It wasn't as if we couldn't afford it. Then when she had a second child she thought I should lend more of a hand. So as the proud father of two girls, I became a bit of a stay-at-home dad. I gave up my offices in Edgware Road and worked from my study at home. After all, I essentially had only one client, our Firm, though it was a bit of an octopus, with its tentacles everywhere.

Usually, in the mornings, I did the school run and I spent time with the kids when they came home in the afternoon. The only concession I made to the gangster life was security. While The Firm did have a lot of notoriety and people were fearful of us, once you are top dog in the underworld, there will always be rivals and the danger of someone trying to overthrow you. So my house was festooned with burglar alarms and surrounded by CCTV, infra-red and motion sensors.

To Vittoria's alarm, I even had a panic room built. She just thought I was overreacting to the crime wave that was sweeping the more affluent areas of West London. With the opening of the film *Absolute Beginners*, Notting Hill had become fashionable. Seen to be affluent, stray burglars began targeting the neighbourhood, but that was not my concern. If some outfit from the East End or south of the river wanted to mount a challenge, I wanted a fortress where I could protect my family if a team of heavies came knocking at the door.

And there was always the police to consider. Vittoria found it unsettling that I had the place regularly swept for listening devices. There was also the possibility of a dawn raid, so I had the doors reinforced. If I was going to be nicked they could at least have the decency to do it during office hours.

As other people knew we had money, they approached us for investment in their criminal ventures. Up until then, we'd never had anything to do with drugs, but we were asked to put some cash into the supply of marijuana. This seemed safe enough. The Flying Squad may be itching to get their hands on us and watching our every move, but we were of no interest to the Drugs Squad – or the National Drugs Intelligence Unit, as they're called.

The problem with weed is transportation. It's bulky and its pungent aroma was difficult to conceal. With sniffer dogs at the airports and patrols at sea, Customs and Excise had succeeded in cutting the smuggling of weed to a trickle. Smokers turned instead to hashish, which is essentially powdered cannabis compressed into a block. Most of it came from Morocco, but pressure was put on the king to restrict the trade. Hashish had also come from Afghanistan, but the Soviet invasion and repeated civil wars cut down the supply, while the competing warlords and insurgents found it much more profitable to cultivate opium instead. Its derivative heroin, again, is far easier to transport and is much more addictive, guaranteeing regular repeat sales. See, it's not just Steve who likes to do his research.

Hashish is usually smoked rolled in a joint with tobacco, which was fast falling out of fashion. If not using joints, you needed pipes and other paraphernalia, which was hard to conceal if the user was raided. With weed, all you needed was regular rolling paper.

Steve was approached by a former weed smuggler whose business was failing. He had a proposition. He wanted us to buy unobtrusive houses in the suburbs. These would be converted into a weed farm. Cannabis plants would be grown hydroponically with their roots in a water-based nutrient solution rather than soil and under UV lights, rather than daylight, twenty-four hours a day. Under these controlled conditions, you not only grow the weed quicker, you produce a stronger version, known on the streets as skunk.

If possible, a house should be found that was near a factory or some other commercial enterprise that used a lot of electricity. That way an enterprising electrician could tap their supply, stealing their power for free. Otherwise, the electrical consumption of a domestic property running UV lights twenty-four hours a day would alert the electric company, if not the authorities.

With this dealt with, there would be little to draw attention to the property. Any comings and goings could be done quietly at night. The curtains would always be closed, but people would get used to that, as long as there was no trouble. After all, people buy properties in London for investment and no one lives in them, so it wouldn't look suspicious.

And for us, we wouldn't need to worry about disguising the true owner of the property. It would be one of our foreign shell companies. According to the paperwork, the house would be rented out to the urban farmer, using a suitable alias. If the place got busted, only the pseudonymous tenant would be liable, and they were unlikely to be found. The property would still belong to us and couldn't be confiscated as the foreign owner ostensibly had nothing to do with what was going on there. For our Firm there would be no risk, just a healthy kickback from the sale of the product.

That's how, albeit at arm's length, we got into the drugs trade.

# CHAPTER SEVENTEEN
## THE SYNDICATE

It seems that news of The Firm's reputation had spread across the Atlantic. A crime syndicate, who had considerable interests in the gaming industry in London, wanted enhanced protection on their casinos, which they thought we could supply as they were seeking to expand their operations. We were happy to oblige and there was a deal to be thrashed out.

Of course, it was not as simple as that. Following the Bank of England heist, the Syndicate thought that we might be getting too big for our boots and could try to muscle in on their action in the West End. A top New York kingpin was sent over. Steve and Mick met him at the Hilton.

There was an element of bluff in this. First came the flattery. The big-time kingpin said that the mob had been keeping an eye on our activities for some time and they were impressed. We were, he said, the nearest thing to a home-grown Mafia that we had in England. There were other gangs, but we were the only one to have an international profile.

If we agreed to help them protect their interests, we would be well paid and there would be sweeteners. The Syndicate had some stolen Canadian bearer bonds that were instantly negotiable. With the Mounties and the FBI on the lookout for them, they were too hot to handle in North America. To get rid of them, they wanted to see whether they could be disposed of on the QT in Europe. Could we help? If we succeeded, this could turn into a lucrative sideline, with them stealing securities in the US and us selling them in the UK or in the EU.

Clearly, given the finance brain it needed, this was one for me. I flew out to Canada where I bought $250,000 worth of bonds at a quarter of the face value. In London and Paris we offloaded them at par, pocketing three-quarters of the take. After that, the traffic in stolen North American securities flourished. With the Syndicate as our sidekicks, we had now entered the big time.

Two more members of the Syndicate came over to see us. They explained that they were organising 'junkets' where American high-rollers would be flown over to gamble in the casinos in the UK. They were investing in new clubs and hotels. Millions of dollars were at stake, so nothing could go wrong. If we could guarantee that there would be no trouble at the new clubs, we could have a percentage. It was a no-brainer.

That was when a gang of French criminals contacted us with a view to also making a closer alliance. They viewed England as an unexploited market. The drugs trade could be doubled overnight, they reckoned. Goods stolen on the Continent could be disposed of here and French gunmen would be available to come if we needed a hit. What they were proposing was a European Union of crime. After all, Europol worked that way, so why shouldn't we?

The Syndicate wanted to see the brothers in New York. Potentially there would be trouble getting visas. People with criminal records are not routinely allowed into the United States. There was an easy way around this. Steve and Mick went to France and applied for visas at the US consulate in Paris who had no way of checking on the criminal records of British subjects.

They then flew from Orly to JFK where US Immigration gave them VIP treatment. No questions were asked and customs did not even examine their bags. This had been laid on by the Syndicate. A Sicilian, who had been the go-between on the stolen securities, was there to meet them.

He drove them into town and checked them into a swanky hotel. The next few days were a round of meetings with legendary gangsters and celebrities. Everything was laid on for them, the full red carpet. Mick was in his element. He loved rubbing shoulders with old-style mobsters. Steve, as always, was more pragmatic. He wanted to get down to business. But the only business on the agenda was further cooperation with criminal groups on the Continent and extending the trade in narcotics in the UK. The Syndicate controlled the import of heroin from the Far East into Europe, so we needed them onside as they ran much of the distribution.

But while there were plenty of powerful people in the rooms they went into, Steve felt cheated as he couldn't get to talk to the top crime bosses, as he had hoped. The truth was that, since the arrest and conviction of John Gotti, the Mafia was not the force it once had been. The *omertà* or code of silence had been broken by Salvatore 'Sammy the Bull' Gravano. He had been given a new identity under the Federal Witness Protection programme for turning state's evidence and testifying against Gotti and his consigliere Frank LoCascio. Both got life and died in prison.

Gravano was not the only one to turn grass. Others followed suit, so the Mafia bosses were careful whom they talked to, even if they were foreigners. A meeting could be set up, they said, but Steve and Mick would have to fly out to Las Vegas. Mick wanted to go. Steve's calmer head prevailed. He trusted no one. Going to New York had been walking into the lion's den, but Las Vegas had been built on Mafia money. It was a step too far – for Steve, at least.

Mick went on to Vegas, where he claimed he did a job for the Colombo family. They wanted someone rubbing out without starting a turf war, so were keen to have an unknown Englishman do it for them. They gave him a photograph of the mark and a .38. Mick said he followed the target to a bar and shot him in the back of the head. It turned out that he was an undercover cop. I'm not sure I believe that. It could be Mick was just boasting.

Mick was not done, though. When he got back to London, he heard that a well-known gambler and club owner who had fallen out with the Mafia was in town. Mick figured he would do the Mafia a favour by rubbing him out. But by the time Mick had got a bomb made, the guy had left the country. Apparently, he was rubbed out by an assassin from the 'Ndrangheta while hiding out in Uruguay.

It turned out that trying to impress the American Mafia was a waste of time. The New York Mafia was a spent force and powerless against the incursions of the Russian Mafia, the Chinese Triads and the Mexican drugs cartels. Perhaps we should have heeded this as a warning, but consoled ourselves with the idea that the gang structure in London was not like that in America. After the bond deals dried up, our connections with the US were at an end.

## CHAPTER EIGHTEEN
### THE DUTCH CONNECTION

Our Firm was now going to go into the drugs trade full-time. Armed robbery was just getting too dangerous, especially with Mick wielding a shooter. Besides, one of Steve's contacts inside the Met seemed to have warned him off. Dealing with drugs you were less likely to be shot down like a dog. We had the contacts and the drug trade soon proved even more lucrative.

Steve regularly visited Amsterdam which had recently been dubbed by a British MEP 'the cesspit of Europe'. Not only was it a haven of pornography and prostitution, it was a major centre for drugs. I would sometimes go over with him. It was not a place to take the wife and kids, as I knew from my stag do there.

There were drugs everywhere. While possessing, processing or selling drugs was illegal in the Netherlands, the authorities distinguished between hard and soft drugs on the grounds that weed and hash posed little risk to health or public order. For the police, time and resources were better spent on heroin, acid and cocaine. Possession of up to thirty grams of cannabis was allowed. Canalside coffee shops made no secret of selling it, even putting a marijuana leaf sign in the window to advertise the fact. They were also listed in the pot smokers' bible the *Golden Blow Guide* and the daily price fixing was announced on pirate radio. Consequently, heads, freaks and dope fiends from around the world were attracted.

As a major port, Amsterdam was a good trans-shipment point. It had an international airport, one of the busiest in Europe, and was less than 50 miles from Rotterdam, Europe's largest seaport. No one was keeping track of how much cannabis was coming in and going out. This alarmed the Netherlands' European neighbours.

Where there is weed, other mind-altering substances are available, though not so openly advertised. This attracted organised crime. LSD, amphetamines and MDMA – that is, Ecstasy – were manufactured in laboratories that were rarely, if ever raided. Heroin came overland via the Balkans from Turkey. Cocaine arrived by ship from South America.

Customs checks were rare and security at Amsterdam's Schiphol Airport was regarded as a joke. And conveniently, the Netherlands borders Belgium, which had strict banking secrecy laws. Back in the 1990s, just over the border there was a town that consisted of three houses, two bars and seven banks – perfect for money-laundering purposes.

With the Big Bang in the City of London now in full swing, the demand for cocaine in the UK soared. Most of it came from Colombia, which was already the biggest supplier of weed to the United States. With the US drug market practically saturated, the Colombians had been eager to get into the UK.

One of the leaders of the Medellín Cartel was married to a Brit. The couple were sent to London to set up a distribution network. They contacted a Czech jewel thief with a German passport who had been on the run since a diamond heist in Munich in 1973, but had good contacts in the underworld here.

He shifted some 400 kilos of coke, paying around £4 million, while his wife spent half a million pounds of the profits on clothes in a month. But he soon got busted. There were fears that he might be killed, so the Met moved him to a police cell in West Yorkshire, but he sawed through the bars of the cell and escaped, never to be seen again.

Meanwhile, his British supplier had been flying hundreds of kilos of Charlie to Florida on a private Cessna, then shipping it to Britain from there. But he got caught in Miami and disappeared into an American jail. His Colombian wife was arrested in the UK and charged with laundering millions of pounds. Six days before her appearance at Knightsbridge Crown Court, she fled, leaving behind a million-pound house in a secluded road in Fulham and £200,000 in bank and building society accounts.

Having lost two major distributors, the Medellín Cartel

resorted to mules, also known as 'stuffers and swallowers', organised mainly by Yardie gangs who largely used women, who secreted the drug consignment in condoms inside their bodies or swallowed it wrapped in cellophane to be recovered in the normal course of events when they got to the UK.

This was dangerous as the packaging might burst, instantly giving the mule an overdose which often proved fatal. Although they were not moving such large quantities as before, there were so many of them that the tide became a flood. Often several were sent on the same plane. If one got caught, the rest would get through. While the price of cocaine on the streets was high, it was cheap to produce, so the losses did not matter – except for the mules who spent time in jail before being deported.

The Medellín Cartel overreached itself when its leader Pablo Escobar got involved in politics. He had the leader of the Liberal Party assassinated and put a bomb on the plane of his successor. But the target missed the plane. The bomb went off, killing 107 people, including two Americans. So the US got involved.

Eventually, Escobar surrendered on the understanding that he would not be extradited to the US. He built his own luxurious prison with a Jacuzzi, a football pitch, unlimited alcohol and visits from hookers. However, he discovered that the authorities planned to send him to a regular jail and escaped. The US then provided Colombian Special Forces with the technology to track him down and Escobar was killed in a gunfight.

As the Medellín Cartel crumbled, the Cali Cartel, also based in Colombia but further south, took over. They came up with a great marketing ploy. Up to that point, cocaine had been expensive and used by rock stars, Wall Street brokers, the former barrow boys in the City and the super-rich. To expand the market, they made coke cheap by getting it cooked up with baking soda, making rocks that were smokable. This form of crack cocaine took over from a brief fashion for free-basing cocaine with ether which often resulted in explosions. Another advantage was that you could make a lot of crack out of relatively little cocaine, so you only had to transport relatively little to make a great deal of product when it reached its destination. Better still, from a business point of view, the instant high smoking crack gave you made it highly addictive. You just had to go back for more. Crack flooded the ghettoes of the US. Next the Cali Cartel turned their attention to the UK where they again aimed to expand the market with poorer people addicted to crack while the better off still sought the kudos of snorting the real thing.

First out of the gate were the remnants of the Richardson gang who had gone up against the Krays in the 1960s. This gave them the sort of reputation that the men in Cali respected.

They had been importing Thai cannabis through Gatwick Airport, paying baggage handlers to remove the suitcases containing the drugs before they reached customs. They then used the same system for the cocaine and seemed to do rather well at it. One consignment of 44 kilos was worth £10 million on the street.

For the Cali Cartel, this was small beer though. They looked into the possibility of bringing a container full of the stuff through Southampton docks. What the Richardsons didn't know was that the police had been teaming up with Customs and Excise and were keeping the gang under surveillance. Again they had the disadvantage of having a high profile in criminal circles.

When a consignment of balsa wood arrived from Ecuador, customs found it had been hollowed out and contained two metric tonnes of cannabis and 154 kilos of cocaine, worth around £40 million. Eddie Richardson, who had already served eleven years for his activities in the 1960s, got another twenty-five for conspiring to import drugs.

This is the dangerous game we were getting into. They were big-time players whose names were known around the world. Steve and Mick were gung-ho – Steve for purely business reasons, Mick because he fancied playing with the big boys. But these guys were serious killers.

# CHAPTER NINETEEN
## THE CALI CARTEL

To handle their exports, the Cali Cartel had set up a front company in Venezuela which would ship enormous consignments of cocaine inside what were ostensibly legitimate goods. Its point man was a young Colombian who settled in the Netherlands and applied for Dutch citizenship. Such a figure would hardly have gone unnoticed by Steve's contacts.

Steve got himself invited down to a meeting at the Atalaya Park hotel outside Puerto Banús, west of Málaga on the Costa del Crime. Colombians and other criminals from Latin America liked to do business in Spain because they didn't need visas and could speak the language. Steve was then taken back to a house in the hills behind Puerto Banús, near Marbella's bullring. The cartel had taken over the place from a Spanish cocaine dealer who owed them money.

It was a large two-storey, stucco-fronted hacienda with a terracotta roof. In the gated driveway there were a collection of Rolls-Royces, Ferraris and Lamborghinis. It boasted an Olympic-sized swimming pool in the back garden. This was surrounded by a dozen beautiful young women sunning themselves in various states of undress. They may not have been wearing much clothing but they were dripping with jewellery. Paying them no mind were a bunch of men playing poker on a card table set up in the shade of an acacia tree.

Steve had a meeting with the cartel's accountant and figured that he should have brought me along. The guy suggested we invested in some of the legitimate businesses the Colombians had recently set up in Spain. If we were investing in legit businesses, Steve would rather do that on our home patch where we could keep an eye on things, rather than abroad where we would have no control. So Steve politely declined, later saying that he wished he'd told them to 'f**k off' but thought it better not to do so in their own backyard.

Present that day was the cartel's new European chief, known as 'the Mexican'. He ran the business from a former monastery 20 miles south of Valencia where he lived with his wife and their two young children. From there and a number of other residential properties in Spain, he arranged drugs shipments from Colombia and huge money transfers to offshore bank accounts. He was interested in what we could offer him, but was suspicious that we might also be trying to do business with the rival Medellín Cartel, who were trying to undercut them and had been contacts in the UK.

Steve was uneasy. He didn't speak Spanish and was alone, surrounded by members of a gang that had a fearsome reputation, all with no backup. Not only was Spain foreign territory, around 60,000 Colombians entered Spain visa-free every year, perfectly legally. It was the only country in Europe that did not require a visa. South American drugs bosses flocked to Madrid, where they were known to have gun battles openly in the streets.

Drug boats from Colombia could no longer make it across the Caribbean which had been closed by the DEA – America's Drug Enforcement Administration. Instead, the cartel's vessels met Spanish trawlers in the mid-Atlantic. Fast launches and smaller fishing boats waited offshore to collect the merchandise and deliver it to the rocky inlets along the deserted coast of Galicia. The mayors and police chiefs of the few towns there were paid off handsomely so the traffic went on unhindered.

Steve knew all about the import routes from the mates he met in the bars around a villa he had recently bought in Fuengirola. Some of them drove up to check the produce when it was stored in the caves and seaside pueblos there, then arranged for it to be collected and driven through France to the Channel ports. Cocaine that could be produced for £1,000 a kilo in Colombia would be sold for £20,000 a kilo in Galicia and be worth £80,000 a kilo on the streets of London.

The problem with this route was that it was overseen by ETA, the Basque separatist movement, who also wanted their cut. Politically motivated, they were arguably even more aggressive than the Colombians. In a seemingly unending war with the government, they wanted money to buy weapons to kill as many Spanish soldiers as possible – and they did not mind killing a few British gangsters along the way.

Because I could speak Spanish, Steve had me flown over. We met with an ETA representative known as The Tigress in the Basque country. During a heated discussion in a hotel room, she pulled a gun. We later learned that she had been involved in twenty-four murders, including the deaths of seventeen members of Spain's Guardia Civil police. It seems we were lucky to escape with our lives.

Clearly The Tigress was far too dangerous to deal with. Instead, Steve managed to make contact with a North African woman who had connections with two senior members of ETA, responsible for fundraising. I think she became his lover, though he never said. But she helped him hammer out a cash-per-shipment deal with ETA. Having lived through the IRA bombing campaign in London, Steve had reservations about dealing with terrorists, but for the moment, we had no choice.

The problem with dealing with ETA was that, along with the Guardia, they had the Grupo Especial de Operaciones or GEO, the anti-terrorist unit, on their tails. Trained by Germany's GSG 9, they were almost as dangerous as the terrorists themselves. Our modest drug-smuggling operation did not merit that much attention. So eventually Steve figured that we could make a better deal if we bought direct from the cartel in South America and asked his contact to arrange a meeting with the leaders in Cali. They seemed to be impressed by our operation and agreed. If we could pull this off, it would be the deal of a lifetime and I was going to be in on it. Steve decided that I had to go with him to Cali as translator.

Naturally, we didn't want the authorities to know what we were up to, so we applied for British visitors' passports which were valid for one year and usable only in Europe. With these in our pockets, we drove to Dover and took the car ferry to France. Our regular passports had been taken out to Paris by courier. From there, we used them to fly out to Colombia.

Arriving in Cali, we were met by a contingent of men carrying automatic weapons. They drove us into the centre of the city where we were taken to an office block. On the fifth floor, after being given the once-over with a handheld scanner to make sure we were not carrying any weapons or listening devices, we were ushered into what looked like the boardroom of a major corporation. There were expensive-looking paintings on the wall and half a dozen men in silk suits were sitting around a huge highly polished mahogany table. All of them were wearing Rolexes of various kinds.

These gentlemen wanted to know what had happened to the consignment that they had sent to the Richardsons. We explained that we had nothing to do with the Richardsons. They were from South London. We were from the west. The

Richardsons were a thing of the past, a hangover from the 1960s. We were the up-and-coming mob. 'What about the Liverpool Mafia and the Yardies?' they asked. They were all very well, we said, if you wanted to deal with the north of England or the Midlands. We were from London. That was where the big money was.

Our hosts then talked among themselves. We seemed to have given the right answers to their questions. If we hadn't, I doubt whether we would have got out of there alive. Not only did they ruthlessly kill junior members of the cartel who made mistakes, they had also undertaken a campaign of 'social cleansing' in Cali. *Desechables* – 'discardables' – such as prostitutes, street children, petty thieves, homosexuals and the homeless were murdered and their bodies dumped in the Cauca River. As useless, potentially rival, gangsters, what chance would we have had?

We were assigned a cartel hitman named 'Popeye' as a minder. He left us for a couple of nights in the Intercontinental to get over our jet lag. Then, just as we were starting to feel normal again, Popeye patted us down again and blindfolded us before driving us to a secret location outside the city. The house was in a secure compound that had armed guards in watchtowers around the perimeter. Once inside the gate, our blindfolds were removed, but it was still a long drive from the gatehouse to the front door of this huge mansion. Inside there was so much gold it was genuinely dazzling. There was also a helipad, a huge pool and a bullring. A matador had been flown in from Spain to entertain a party our hosts were planning. There were also a number of rare and exotic animals in the gardens. A tiger was pacing in a cage, but the rest – everything from capybaras to spider monkeys – were roaming around freely.

Our hosts were polite and generous. They were not best pleased that we were planning to risk importing cocaine in bulk direct into the UK as the Richardsons had, rather than using the tried-and-tested route through Galicia, but they had been following our activities and showed us a certain respect. As it was, they were gracious enough to entertain us. I think they were trying to get our measure. Besides, the plans we had would also increase the profits for them and relieve them of the tiresome business of arranging transportation.

One of the top men in the cartel wanted to practise his English, so he kept us around as much as possible. He flew us in his helicopter out to Cartagena, where his yacht was moored and we sailed to Aruba. A number of influential people were on board the yacht, along with a bevy of beautiful girls including an ex-Miss Colombia. Among the party were a number of Turkish and Italian heroin traffickers.

After this trip, he took us on a private plane to an airstrip in the Colombian jungle where he showed us one of this drug processing plants. We heard that he had $900 million buried in the jungle around the factory. The money was brought back from the United States in specially partitioned water tankers. The Colombians had the same problem we did – how to deal with all that money.

Out there in the rainforest, it would have been pretty easy to bump us off. In Amazonia, life is cheap. Nobody would have been any the wiser. We'd never be missed. Everyone in the encampment worked for the cartel and they were all armed. We were not. They'd made sure of that. A couple of shots in the back of the head would have done the job. And there would be no problem disposing of the bodies. The armies of maggots and other creepy-crawlies would strip the flesh from the bones in a matter of days. In hot humid conditions even the bones decay.

But no one made so much as a threatening move. Clearly we could trust our hosts and they trusted us. So it was out there in the jungle that we made a deal to import 1,000 kilos of cocaine into the UK. Then we returned to England, the way we came, showing our visitors' passports so, as far as the British authorities were concerned, we hadn't been outside Europe. The regular ten-year passports we'd used for the trip to Colombia followed in the post.

Then we got down to business, setting up a company to import scrap metal from South America, our cover for the new imports. After numerous transatlantic phone calls, Steve arranged to import 40 tonnes of aluminium and 85 tonnes of lead in ingots three foot by three foot square. Inside each of the huge bars of lead there would be a steel box containing cocaine. Lead was impervious to X-rays and so thick that, unless you knew exactly where to drill, you'd never find the secret compartment. The lead was not soft like that used on roofing, but hard like the lead used to make bullets, and it would burn out most drill bits, so there was very little chance of whoever was trying to check them getting lucky.

The Cali Cartel had already set up an export office in Caracas. I flew out to Venezuela, again via Paris, to oversee the departure of the drugs. The cartel's front company sorted out the paperwork and the container containing the ingots were loaded on to a ship. At the Dominican Republic, the container was unloaded and put on a ship bound for Piraeus in Greece, but making a stop at Felixstowe. The Caracas front company had also set up a corporate bank account in Amsterdam where we had to make a down payment of £4 million. When the drugs reached British soil, we would have to pay the balance via their bank in Holland. One can only imagine the consequences if we did not.

But when the shipment arrived, Customs and Excise were waiting. It seems the authorities had had a tip-off. We never discovered the source. They took one of the ingots and tried to drill into it. But thankfully the drill bit was too short to penetrate the hidden box and snapped inside the lead. So they gave up and started examining the container itself, figuring the drugs must be hidden there. They found nothing.

After a couple of weeks, the container was cleared by customs. Transportation was organised by Mick. The container was taken by rail and lorry to a lock-up he had rented in Harlesden. A specialist who knew how to remove the cocaine from the lead ingots had flown over from Colombia. Each ingot weighed two tonnes and had to be lifted several feet off the floor so someone could get underneath to cut away the lead and reach the steel box inside. For that we needed a heavyweight forklift truck.

Once the cocaine was removed, Mick was left with a heap of scrap lead, which we left under a mound of rubble. Eventually, it was dug up and sent to a yard in Newcastle-upon-Tyne where it was melted down.

The cocaine had been bought for £14,000 a kilo, rather than £20,000 on the Galician coast, and could be cut and sold on the streets for around £80,000 a kilo. That would give us a profit of at least £70 million. As The Firm's only money man, I was going to be busy and I found a new way to get money out of the country – buying top-end cars and shipping them abroad. Flashing the cash around car dealerships had its own problems, but most people in the motor trade knew that our firm was not to be messed with.

# CHAPTER TWENTY
## LAW AND DISORDER

As soon as the first shipment had been distributed, a second was on its way. This time, 900 kilos, worth £150 million on the streets, was on the high seas. It would be inside thirty-two cylindrical ingots bound for Felixstowe. While we got away with the first one easily enough, this time didn't go so smoothly.

First, the cartel's front company in Caracas was shut down by the Venezuelan authorities. Next, the Dutch police raided a warehouse and caught the Colombian specialist wearing gloves and goggles, drill in hand opening an ingot. There were thirty-five in the warehouse bound for an outfit in Germany. Thirty-seven packets of cocaine were recovered, containing a total of 945 kilos. More than our entire second shipment.

During the three weeks our shipment was on the high seas, the Cali Cartel's European sales manager was arrested in Holland while arranging another 800-kilo shipment and was charged with conspiracy to import drugs. The whole business was falling apart.

We got a call from the cartel telling us that the consignment to Felixstowe would have to be sacrificed. Security had been compromised by the arrest in Holland. As the fault was on their side, they would take the hit, but we would lose our deposit.

Customs intercepted the shipment. They had now worked out how to open the ingots. They found twenty-eight or twenty-nine packages in each ingot – 905 kilos in all with a purity of between 80 and 90 per cent. But then the police took over the operation. They sealed the ingots up again and waited to see if anyone was dumb enough to come and collect them.

Indeed, they were. The guys we'd hired to pick up what they thought was an innocent shipment of the scrap metal went. I guess Mick hadn't warned them. As far as they were concerned, what they were picking up was just lead. When one of them was searched, it was found that he was carrying Mick's phone number.

At six in the morning an armed police team burst into Mick's flat. They found him in bed with his girlfriend and arrested him. In return, they got a right mouthful. One of the cops wrote down what he was saying. When Mick was asked to sign the cop's notebook, admitting what he had written was a true account, Mick said: 'How can I sign your notebook with my hands cuffed behind my back, you c**t?'

In Mick's flat, the police found £10,000 in cash, a Bearcat scanning device for intercepting police frequencies and a mobile phone bearing the number of the transportation company that had gone to pick up the ingots. He was taken to West End Central in Savile Row.

It looked like the cozzers had Mick banged to rights. If they had him, we were all in trouble. Always a loose cannon, he was also a loose thread. Pull him and our whole operation would come unravelled. If the police liaised with the cops in the Netherlands who had nicked the cartel's man in Europe, or flew out to Venezuela and talked to those involved with the front company in Caracas, they would have me and Steve too.

But we got lucky. From the prosecution evidence that Mick's brief got his hands on, the police had employed a grass who had been given a reward of £100,000. He had supplied the date of the shipment's arrival at Felixstowe and details of its storage and transportation onwards without telling Customs and Excise who were not happy. They suspected that the informant had only grassed because he had a rival operation and aimed to knock out the competition.

Since no drugs had been recovered from the first shipment, the police couldn't prove that there had been a shipment at all. The second shipment had not reached us and only Mick had been implicated. But customs figured that the police informant had also profited royally from the first shipment, so it would be unjust, if not immoral, to give him immunity from prosecution.

They raided the informant's house and noticed a bulge in the ceiling. In the loft, they found twelve holdalls containing £1,759,210. In his bedroom they found another 1.1 million in Swiss francs, worth around £500,000. If that was not good enough, when they tested the notes, they were contaminated with cocaine.

They also busted his business, a car dealership. The ledgers showed evidence of money laundering. The police were far from happy. They had lost their star witness. On the instructions of the Attorney General, the charges against the informant were dropped and he fled the country.

This left the prosecution case looking decidedly threadbare. There was no evidence to suggest that Mick had set up the drugs shipment. Steve and I had done that and the police were not prosecuting us, so any evidence to that effect was deemed inadmissible.

Before any defence witnesses had been called, the judge ruled that the prosecution had presented insufficient evidence for a conviction and instructed the jury to acquit. As Mick left the court, he smiled and waved at the police. He was on his way to spend his £170,000 – that is, his share after I had put it through the international spin cycle.

His acquittal made him a hero in the neighbourhood. He drove around in an open-topped Lexus so that he could acknowledge his fans. Somehow, whenever Mick fell in the shit, he came up smelling of roses. Meanwhile, the authorities took their eye off the ball. Their time was consumed in compiling a report into how the police and customs between them had screwed up.

For us, the case was a godsend. The evidence presented in court against Mick provided us with every detail of how the authorities operated against us. We would be more careful next time. As the ancient Chinese military philosopher Sun Tzu said, know your enemy. Or rather, in *The Art of War*, he wrote: 'If you know the enemy and know yourself, you need not fear the result of a hundred battles. If you know yourself but not the enemy, for every victory gained you will also suffer a defeat. If you know neither the enemy nor yourself, you will succumb in every battle.'

Just because I had been lured into a life of crime did not mean I had given up reading. In fact, the excessive profits left me more time for the appreciation of literature and art.

The Home Office's report into the inquiry was also illuminating. It seemed that, years before, customs officers had uncovered corruption in the Met's drug squad. This gave customs a moral superiority and they lobbied to take pole position in the fight against drugs. They had a superior intelligence operation and were, at least, they contended, honest.

In an interdepartmental turf war, the police fought back. The Home Office then decided that responsibility for the war on narcotics should be split. Customs were tasked with stopping the importation of drugs. They were to stop the shipments as they arrived and bust suspects at the ports and airports. The police were to track down any drugs that got through and arrest the gangs who financed the trade and distributed the stuff.

For us, the continued enmity between the police and customs was a barrel of laughs. The result was customs found themselves arresting undercover cops and vice versa, while both sides claimed the kudos for big busts and the credit for the same seizures. Customs took the mickey calling the police 'Oscar Bravo', the phonetic abbreviation for 'Old Bill' – which is what we called them – while the police dismissed customs as the 'baccy guards' who should be spending their time checking duty-frees.

With this farce being played out, it was easy for us to become complacent. We needed to remember that, not just Mickey but all of us had nearly got busted were it not for the intervention of good luck and bad blood between Plod and HM Customs and Excise – the boys who brought you VAT. We needed to reorganise our operation again and Steve decided we needed to adopt a cell structure, as terrorists did. He didn't like working with them, but he appreciated their structures.

Cells of three or four people would carry out missions.

Each person would have their essential role – intelligence, transport, security, logistics. That way, if the cell got caught, they would not bring the whole structure down. A grass would only be able to rat on the two or three people he worked most closely with and would have little information on what the rest of the organisation was up to. It was the way the Cali Cartel worked. They were masters of insulated cells, employing an army of surrogates responsible for every detail of the trafficking business, from car rental to pager and phone purchase, from the storage of cocaine in safe houses to the keeping of inventory and accounts.

While I was an accountant and Steve could pass as a businessman owning a string of pubs, clubs, restaurants and other businesses, we needed some plausible cover for Mick, something legitimate to put on his tax returns and explain how he made a living to any policeman who may be interested – and they were interested. So he became a 'security consultant', providing doormen and the heavies at concerts and boxing matches. It suited a man of his build and temperament, and he recruited a bunch of burly bouncers we could call on for any criminal enterprise we were planning.

The Firm also supplied the doormen at clubs. These were important as they controlled the sale of drugs inside, though this was chicken feed. While we controlled the importation of drugs, we didn't want to get our hands dirty at street level.

The money is not so good down there. As the book *Freako-nomics* points out, the majority of drug dealers live with their mothers because they make so little money they can't afford to live anywhere else.

As wholesalers, we supplied the 'Ten Kilo Men' who were the local drug bosses whose gangs often depended on family ties. Sometimes there were rivalries between them that led to bloodshed. Mick would keep the peace and settle any disputes. He had such a fearsome reputation that no one crossed him. You had to be a bit tasty to take him on, otherwise you'd be in for a right good spanking.

When he went around the estates where the Top Boys ruled the roost and controlled the trade in drugs – or 'food' as they called it – he could leave his car with the windows open and the keys in the ignition and no one would touch it. He didn't often resort to violence. His reputation was that solid. It was enough to put the frighteners on. He would never let even the smallest debt go unpaid.

We knew that the police would be happy to put us all behind bars, but their resources were not limitless, so it was Mick they concentrated on. He was often followed. He switched cars regularly to make this more difficult. Phone calls had to be kept short and vague. Mick also kept a sharp eye out for perceived traitors.

But the law did have its successes. There was a small travel agent in Notting Hill Gate that ran coach trips to Amsterdam. The bus would leave late on Friday night and return forty-eight hours later. This gave travellers time to sample the attractions of the bars, coffee shops and, if they were that way inclined, the red-light district.

One of our guys would be on board and bring back speed and Ecstasy from the factories in the Netherlands. On one occasion, he had been on such a bender the night before that he missed the coach, so had to drive down to Gatwick to grab a flight to Schiphol. When the bus returned the next day, he was on it. At Dover, the passengers were disembarked for a passport check, but still rather hung-over he left the bags containing the drugs on board. The Customs and Excise team boarded the bus, found the bags and seized around 950,000 pills with a street value of at least £6 million.

The courier admitted everything and got six years, but the police also nicked the 65-year-old owner of the travel agency that organised the trips who had nothing to do with the smuggling operation. Although he denied everything, he was given eighteen years at Maidstone Crown Court. He served nine, but never gave up his fight to clear his name. Though he was not on our payroll, we paid for his lawyers. Finally, three years after he was released, his conviction was overturned by the Court of Appeal who found that material that would've been vital to the defence was not disclosed by the Crown at the trial.

Another coach was stopped with 400 tabs of Ecstasy and 14 kilos of heroin worth up to £2 million in a secret compartment accessed from under a rear seat and leading under the toilet compartment. These mixed batches were called 'groupage' loads. By then, we had gone into the business of being 'placers'. That is, we took orders from the distributors – they placed orders with us. If you wanted a tonne of cocaine, we would bring in a tonne of cocaine. If you wanted 50 kilos of cannabis, that's what you'd get. You got it, sold it and paid up. If the shipment was lost anywhere along the line, we'd still get paid. Mick made sure of that. Then again, if anyone got caught we'd cut them off and never deal with them again. Even if they had not been turned by the cops to get a lighter sentence, they were still a security risk.

The occasional bust did not have much impact on our business. Even if one in three shipments was lost, we would still make plenty. But our strike rate was better than that. Customs and Excise held up one coach for inspection, suspecting that there were drugs on board. They gave it a thorough search but found nothing and had to let it go. In fact, there were 100 kilos of heroin hidden in the chassis, which we sold on in forty-eight hours.

Being a customs officer must be a thankless task. I'd guess that they only seized about 10 per cent of the drugs we were bringing in. The police picked up another 1 per cent, but 89 per cent got through. Every batch that made it to shore was a victory that put a smile on our faces. Within hours, the drugs would be gone. The only thing the cozzers could do then was to try and catch the dealers, the small fry. Busting kids selling small packets on the street didn't give them much satisfaction, though. It hardly stemmed the tide.

The only other way to put us out of business was to trace the money. It was my job to frustrate them. I don't want to give away too many tricks of the trade, but the United Nations report on the 'World Drug Problem' of 1998 spelt out the basics of money laundering and explains the three stages:

'Placement. The initial entry of funds into the financial system serves the purpose of relieving the holder of large amounts of actual cash and positioning these funds in the financial system for the next stage. Placement is the most vulnerable stage of the process, as the chance of discovery of the illicit origin of the money is greatest at the beginning.

'Layering. The next stage describes a series of transactions designed to conceal the money's origin. At this level money is often sent from one country to another and then broken up into a variety of investments, which are moved frequently to avoid detection.

'Integration. In this stage, the funds have been fully assimilated into the legal economy where they can be used for any purpose.'

One of the routes we used involved that bureau de change we owned at arm's length in Notting Hill Gate. It proved so popular that other gangs were also using it, which was great because we got a cut of each transaction. The problem was finding enough high value foreign notes. The manager would have to phone around other bureaux and a courier had to be dispatched to get them from Thomas Cook or wherever. It became such big business, I wondered how long we could keep it secret. But with customs and the Old Bill chasing each other's tail, I figured it would be safe for a while longer. Our guys were used to keeping their eyes peeled from the armed robbery game. If it came under surveillance they would have spotted it. In this case, I was wrong.

# CHAPTER TWENTY-ONE
## SECURITY

There were other problems on the horizon. It began when one of Mick's bouncers threw a troublemaker out of a club. The guy cursed and said he would come back and take his revenge. The bouncer had heard it all before and paid it no mind. But the guy was not kidding. He came back with a gun and shot the doorman. The incident was caught on CCTV. The police recognised the gunslinger and he got fifteen years.

We all hoped that it stopped there. But the police used it as an excuse to crack down on the security firms as they suspected the doormen were involved in drug dealing and protection rackets. Twelve people were arrested and charged with supplying drugs, demanding money with menaces, extortion, arson, kidnapping and witness intimidation.

This threw everything up in the air. The market for door work was now wide open and rival security firms were fighting for space. And customers were still giving trouble. A couple of months later, a family started cutting up rough in a nightclub. One of Mick's bouncers tried to throw them out. There was a fight and one of the family was floored. The family carried the unconscious man out, again swearing that they would have their revenge.

Soon, the bouncer was getting out of a car with Mick when two men appeared with guns and started shooting at them. The shooters ran and got away unscathed. It seemed a full-scale door war was brewing and Mick started refusing to go anywhere unless he was tooled up.

In a seemingly unrelated incident, a 24-year-old man was walking home at night through Shepherd's Bush when he was blasted in the back with a shotgun. Members of Voytek's gang were suspected. They were still smarting from the attack Mick had organised years before. One of them was arrested and held in custody for thirteen months before the charges were dropped.

And that was when Voytek re-emerged. It seems that he'd recently taken over a club in the area where the victim's cousins and brothers were regulars. They were barred. In an attempt to sort the situation out, a senior member of the family, a former professional boxer, offered to undertake a 'straightener' where the matter would be sorted out man to man. Voytek accepted the challenge and a fight was arranged.

Although he fancied himself as a tough nut, Voytek found himself flat on his back. Under the rules of the straightener, it should have ended there. But Voytek was not prepared to lose face and accept defeat. The rumour circulated that his opponent had a knuckleduster concealed under the leather gloves he wore. The following day, he was just getting out of his car in front of his house when a man stepped from a parked car and shot him. He survived. The gunman was never caught, but the rumour was that it was Voytek.

Tragically, it didn't end there. After the wounded man went back to work, he was driving home from work when a car stopped in front of him with two men in it. He got out of his car and walked over to remonstrate. Harsh words were exchanged. One of the men then pulled a gun and shot him. They drove off, leaving the victim dead in the road.

The following day, petrol was poured through the door of the club where it had all begun and it was burned to the ground. That was followed by random shootings. Six houses in the area were sprayed with bullets.

I was more than ever grateful that I had upped the security on the house, despite Vittoria's misgivings. Now I figured it was time to invest in bulletproof glass for windows. I had considered moving out for a while, but I figured it was safer to stay where we were where we at least had some protection.

Knowing that he was chief suspect for the murder, Voytek went to the police station voluntarily and denied any knowledge of the killing. His alibi held up and, a few days later, he flew to Poland to spend time with his family there. A couple of members of his gang were also suspected. The police held them for questioning for a couple of days, then released them without charge.

With Voytek out of the picture, you'd have thought that things would have quietened down. They didn't. Voytek was spending his time in Poland making criminal contacts and recruiting new soldiers which he was sending over. They brought with them illegal handguns that were widely available in former Eastern Bloc countries now that the security forces had been disbanded.

Soon, it was like the Wild West on the streets. Armed police began coming out more and more, and there was a policy of stop and search for anyone who looked dodgy. Cars were stopped and suspects were made to get out and lie on the ground. It was no good for any of us. The whole criminal community was under siege. Our usual live-and-let-live understanding with the police was thrown out of the window and we could not go about our everyday business. Usually they would turn a blind eye on our minor peccadillos. Now there was nothing the boys could get away with.

The police had some successes, seizing caches of guns and ammunition, and the shootings began to tail off when a couple of faces pulled long sentences for possession. Others fled the country to Jamaica or to seek refuge in Eastern Europe.

Knowing that he was a target from both sides of the legal divide, Mick took to wearing body armour. He avoided trouble by not carrying a gun on the streets, though everyone knew there were plenty he could put his hands on if needs be. Nevertheless, the police suspected he was behind some of the killings and he was hauled in for questioning multiple times. He played it cool. One of the more disturbing stories that did the rounds was that he had helped two of the gunmen escape to the West Indies. Once there, they had asked for more money to start a new life. He paid to have them slotted instead. Their bodies were never found.

We had a family meeting and Steve and I persuaded Mick that things might calm down on the streets if he made himself scarce for a bit. So he bought an executive home near to Epsom Downs racecourse with a flagstone patio, large garden with its own sprinkler system, a filtered pond with Koi carp in it, a top-of-the-range burglar alarm system, naturally, spacious rooms with pinewood floors and Persian rugs and a discreet Peugeot in the garage.

But such a downmarket motor would not be good enough for long. He soon swapped it for a black Lexus. To fill his time, he decided to learn to fly a helicopter, possibly because he saw posh people landing on Epsom Downs to watch the Derby and other races. There was a training school at Redhill Aerodrome ten miles away. It cost him £500 an hour. He mastered the practical skills of flying, but failed the written test, which involved more reading than he could cope with.

After the London end of a Turkish gang that were bringing in morphine from the Middle East were busted, Steve sent Mick out to Holland to re-establish the Turkish connection. He was also to find new labs making MDMA as the demand for Ecstasy in the clubs was soaring.

With control of the door, in one club we could give five dealers their own pitch. Each of them would sell about two hundred tabs a night at £10 a pop. That's a turnover of £10,000 a day. It was easier than ever to bring E in from the Continent since the Channel Tunnel had been opened, but there were also now new labs in Wales synthesising it so we could ship it in without bothering about customs. This was a vital backup after an articulated lorry was stopped making a transhipment of 150,000 tabs of MDMA, 110 kilos of amphetamine and 80 kilos of cannabis, which was seized at a service station on the M20.

Thankfully, we had managed to re-establish our connections in South America and began cooking up crack. The business was soon making £20,000 a week, that's over £1 million a year. Others were making money out there. With business booming, old-time enmities were dropped. Or rather, they dropped down a level. It was now the kids on their mountain bikes selling it on the estate who wore full-face balaclavas and bulletproof vests.

We also went into the export business. Two of our lads had been out in Australia and found out that E selling for

£10–£12 on the streets in London would fetch £25–£40 there. And they could do much better than that. We would supply them at wholesale prices from the UK after they set up two front companies that ostensibly exported footwear.

They bought ladies' shoes that were boxed here and sent to Australia. In the heels, there was a compartment containing drugs. They would pay for the drugs by making regular deposits of cash in banks in Australia for transfer of the money back to England. These sums would be around £4,500, just below the A$10,000 limit set by the Australian Transaction Reports Act. Any cash transaction over that amount had to be reported.

The names of the senders and recipients varied, along with the exact amount of money. Once in the UK, the money was shuffled around various bank accounts, through the client accounts of a firm of solicitors with cash transfers to the post office and travel agencies.

Their front companies then invested their profits in property, including apartments in a high-rise block that overlooked Sydney Harbour. They had money in false names in bank accounts all over Australia. It all fell apart when one of them got arrested with 30,000 fake Ecstasy tablets. He bolted across Bondi Beach in his underpants and made it back to England on a false passport. The other was caught by customs at Sydney Airport with 2 kilos of the drug in the false bottom in his suitcase.

# CHAPTER TWENTY-TWO
## THE HOOK OF HOLLAND

In the Netherlands, Mick had rented a villa outside the village of Warmond, about halfway between Amsterdam and the Hook of Holland, another convenient port with ferry links to Harwich. The house stood back from the main road behind a hedge and a small dyke. The front and sides of the house were sheltered by tall trees. To the rear, there were miles of tulip beds and flat farmland which he regularly scanned with his powerful binoculars.

In the house, he had a large flat-screen TV and a laptop to conduct his business, but little else. He had a mobile phone, of course, but he tried not to use it much in case the authorities were listening. He was reasonably confident that the local police had no idea who he was, but if he called a UK number there was always a chance that the Met would be monitoring the call. Even so, Steve and I heard from him regularly, though the calls avoided any talk of business.

Warmond was in easy reach of Amsterdam by road or rail. He would go into the city most nights to conduct his business and, without the girlfriend he'd left behind in his flat in Mayfair, visit a brothel. With the cash at his disposal, he could afford the best. Sometimes he was entertained by several hookers at a time, or so he told us. There was no detail that he did not share.

I guess it must have been kinda lonely despite all the female company. At night, he liked to phone up from some high-class massage parlour to gloat about what a good time he was having. He'd call from a Jacuzzi and you could hear the clink of glasses and the girls giggling in the background.

When you went over to visit, Mick liked to show you round his haunts. One of them was a veritable palace, not far from one of the Dutch Royal Family's many royal residences. It had rooms overlooking a blue swimming pool and a glitzy bar with a pole and glammed-up girls who charge €300 an hour. Mick had got to know the girls well and they would come over to the villa if he phoned. Again, I think I should leave it there.

But Mick never let his pleasure interfere with his work. His motto was that women were for the night. The day was devoted to business and the consignments from Holland kept on coming. There were slip-ups. A batch of heroin from Pakistan concealed in table lamps was stopped by the Dutch police. Seven men were convicted when customs found a large haul of cannabis concealed in a secret compartment welded to the exhaust system of a lorry. But the supply of drugs continued as the business was profitable enough to recruit new smugglers. They knew what they were getting into and were paid well. We even helped out their wives and kids if they got caught and went to jail.

Mick set up a small corps of gofers so that he wouldn't have to conduct business on the phone. Messages would be conveyed by word of mouth. He also travelled widely, particularly around Belgium, France, then on to Turkey, so he could conduct business face to face. Several times, he visited Sofia to meet the bosses of the Eastern European drugs clans. He would take a bodyguard with him in his Jag. Jaguars were uncommon in post-communist Bulgaria. He was stopped by the police, who decided to search the car for contraband. When nothing was found, Mick and his bodyguard were told they were free to go, but they found the car in bits and had no way of putting it back together again.

Even though the king of Morocco was having another crackdown on drugs, Mick somehow managed to get 500 kilos of hash out. At that time, a lot of filming was being done in southern Spain and Morocco. Mick used a front company that hired out TV, electrical and sound equipment to film crews. Trucks carried the gear back and forth to the Costa del Sol, then onwards by ferry from Algeciras to Tangier.

Unfortunately, the guy running the operation could not keep his mouth shut. All the undercover cops had to do was follow him to his local boozer to hear him, after a few pints, bragging about drug smuggling and the huge amounts of money involved.

He was bringing back a lorry carrying banks of video screens when a joint team of police and customs officers pounced. They searched the truck and found nothing. While they were scratching their heads, one over-zealous customs officer examined one of the backs of the TV screens. Something looked wrong to him and he began prising one open. The rest of the team went mental. There's hell to pay if you begin damaging legitimate property.

As it turned out, he was right. Inside each unit there was a specially constructed box containing the drugs that would allow the TV set to work without damaging the goods. Five hundred kilos of cannabis were seized and the loudmouthed trucker got six years.

This was another valuable supply route cut off from us. But as it had been organised remotely by Mick in Holland, there was nothing to connect it to The Firm. When the stuff did get through, we just took the profits from wholesale and distribution.

But Mick was well connected. He always found a new source of supply. And he was turning into something of a businessman. He bought cannabis, heroin and cocaine whole-sale, then sold it on with a 500 per cent mark-up to criminal gangs who wanted to ship it on themselves to the UK where they would make a similar mark-up. Otherwise, if they wanted us to arrange the shipping, they would have to pay a £25,000 handling fee. Mick would then pay coach operators or hauliers £500 a kilo for carrying cannabis or £1,500 a kilo for powder. What's more, we handled so much of the supply that we could control the price on the street.

What I didn't like about his operation was that he had taken on a number two – a wide boy from Manchester named Mike Janson. They shared similar tastes and snorted coke together. According to his own account, Janson had an impressive CV in criminal activity and had some contacts of his own in Latin America. I met him when I went over to discuss the figures with Mick. It was a frequent occurrence as we were loath to write anything down and the means of communication were anything but secure. I did not trust him one bit. I did not like having someone who was not family so closely tied into The Firm. With Mick handling imports, Steve dealing with wholesale and distribution and me doing the laundering, we were now equal partners.

This meant that, if anything went wrong, I would be serving a long sentence beside them. Once, I had had ambitions to be a humble accountant. Now I was a kingpin in an international drug-smuggling operation and risked the quiet life I'd enjoyed with my wife and daughters, and everything I valued.

# CHAPTER TWENTY-THREE
## THE FIX

Dad had been ill, so they let him out early on compassionate grounds. Given the state of his health, he was unlikely to resume his career as a burglar or an armed robber. He wasn't going to be running across the pavement soon, or anywhere else. He moved in with Mum in Bexhill and contented himself with a leisurely retirement. Steve made sure that Mum and Dad wanted for nothing.

Life had been moving on. Steve and Maureen had a second child, a daughter. They would come over to the house in Notting Hill on Sundays and the children would play together in the garden. One afternoon Mick joined us. He thought he would take the risk to pay a flying visit to see the old man. There was also a score he wanted to settle. A Polish geezer had been jumping his old woman – not that Mick had time for her any more, but he considered this disrespect. Besides, he was not having any Pole taking liberties, especially as he had heard that Voytek was back in town. He hit the guy so hard that his hand swelled up and he had to go to hospital to get a tetanus shot. Otherwise, he was in and out of England in the blink of an eye, a week tops, and without the authorities being any the wiser.

Now safely back in Holland, Mick was getting lax. I guess because the Dutch police had showed no interest in him, he thought he was untouchable, and so he began breaking his own rules. One night he was balling out a contact back home for using his home phone to make a sensitive call, seemingly unaware that he was prone to do the same thing and talk unadvisedly on an open line.

Meanwhile things got worse. The door wars had died down, but then a local lad had got drunk in a club and argued with the doorman over a £5 entrance fee. He smashed a bottle and waved the broken neck about. Punches were thrown and he was chucked out.

As the guy was getting up from the pavement, he pulled a gun, pointed at the doorman and pulled the trigger. There was a click, but it didn't go off. He tried again. Another click. Realising the gun wasn't going to fire, he turned on his heels and ran off, pursued by two bouncers.

He got unlucky. As he turned the corner, he ran straight into two constables who were writing out parking tickets. They took no notice of him, but he waved the gun at them anyway. Apparently they fancied themselves as heroes. Taking no notice of the firearm, they grabbed him even though he kept on pulling the trigger. At the police station, the two doormen gave statements and he was charged with two counts of attempted murder.

The lad's father knew Mick and phoned him to see what he could do. Mick knew the doormen. They were on his firm and he tried to get them to withdraw their statements. They refused. They were not going to stand in a club door and have some punk wave a gun in their faces. Nothing doing.

Mick figured that they would calm down after a couple of days and that they'd reconsider. He offered them money. They refused that too, saying they'd lose their credibility if they let this go. Besides, the police had seen everything. They caught the guy running down the street, waving a gun with the two bouncers running after him. One of the cops even said he had been shot at. Whatever happened, there was going to be no happy ending.

It was then that Mick broke cover and called Steve to talk about it. Steve said he would see what he could do. He had contacts.

It turned out that the gun was a replica, but someone had bored out the barrel so, in theory, it could have fired. But the first bullet got stuck in the barrel. When he pulled the trigger a second time, the whole mechanism jammed. So even if he claimed it wasn't a real gun, the police might bring a lesser charge, but he was not going to get off scot-free.

Even if they had a sympathetic insider in the police station, the gun couldn't just go missing from any strongroom. However, Steve's man said that one of the policemen had screwed up his statement and he thought that he could get his hands on the others, so perhaps a deal could be made.

Steve called Mick and told him the good news that he had an agent of influence in the case and could fix it. The next day, the police station was raided by officers from A10, the anti-corruption unit. Those on the case were questioned and files were taken away. Steve immediately suspected that Plod must have tapped at least one of their phones and were exerting undue influence on someone inside the investigation.

In the UK, the police cannot use evidence picked up from phone taps in court cases. Besides, they needed permission for a phone tap from the Home Secretary and it was rarely given except in cases of terrorism. The Dutch police had no such restraints.

The case against the gunman got so convoluted that, in the end, it was dropped. So we had a result. It was not until sometime later I discovered who Steve's inside man was. It was Vittoria's brother Alex.

It was not that he was a bent cop – well, not any more bent than the rest of the Flying Squad. I knew that Steve was a Free-mason, but I did not know Vittoria's brother was on the square too. He had been inducted by her father who, apparently, was pretty high up in the lodge. I understood now why Steve and Vittoria's brother were so matey at the wedding reception. I guess they'd exchanged funny handshakes or whatever they do.

All he had to do was carelessly screw up the paperwork. Evidence can be lost. Documents can be misplaced. Stories can get confused after a time. Testimony can be disputed, particularly when it has been picked over repeatedly and a less than watertight case can be put to the Crown Prosecution Service. The CPS are loath to go ahead with a case unless they are certain to get a conviction.

Anyway, Steve was now in Vittoria's brother's debt, though it was probably best to wait until Christmas to buy him a drink. I'm not sure where that left me though. Once again, I had been bound more tightly into this web of criminality. But that was only a minor consideration. The big problem now was how much the Dutch police had overheard – and how much had they shared with Scotland Yard which might bring our entire operation tumbling down?

# CHAPTER TWENTY-FOUR
## BUSTED

In Holland, Mick provided a safe haven for other criminals on the run from the law in the UK. Principal among them was Mike Janson, his Manc sidekick who said he had taken his alias from a gravestone. But there were other local boys from the Smoke who had got themselves into a bit of bother, including one heavyweight armed robber who had done the £1.5 million raid on a cash depot in Slough, using a flat-bed truck to smash through the loading bay and into the vault.

Most of them lived in a house Mick rented for them in the village of Waverveen, ten miles south of Amsterdam. Built on a polder, which is low-lying reclaimed land, it was surrounded for miles by flat, featureless fields, making it impossible to spy on. Or so they thought.

One day, a couple of them were out fishing in a nearby canal when they were approached by a local angler. The Brits were keen fishermen and spotted that the man who approached them was using the wrong type of bait. They told Mick, who dismissed their concerns as he was still convinced that the police had no idea where he was or what they were up to. He did not realise that they were closing in on him.

While he didn't pay heed to this instance, he was very conscious of another potential breach of security. One of Mick's rules was that the guys he put up in Waverveen should not burden themselves with girlfriends. Women caused problems and could not be depended on when it came to security. In spite of this rule, one of them fell for a beautiful girl from Moldova. She was married with a child, but her husband agreed to let her go and work as a prostitute in Amsterdam to pay for an operation their son badly needed. She and Mick's mate could barely keep their hands off each other and she tagged along even when the guy was working. Mick bitched about it constantly when I went over to see him.

At the time, Mick was preoccupied by a big cocaine deal he and Mike were setting up with the Cali Cartel through a contact in Bogotá. The intermediary wanted the money up front, but the amounts involved even stretched our long lines of credit in Amsterdam to the limit. Once again, the coke would be shipped as scrap metal in ingots, but this time they would be arriving in Holland.

This was not the only deal we had going at the time. More cannabis was coming in from Spain, but under pressure from the EU, the Spanish authorities were cracking down on trafficking. Mick had to resort to getting the gear carried over the Pyrenees by couriers with backpacks, stopping at youth hostels and mountain huts along the way.

The problem was that, due to the weather conditions in the mountains, the hash was not arriving in France in good condition. Mick had to go out to Spain to show his guys there how to wrap it properly. I guess Mick must have started using coke by then. And by that, I mean overusing it. He was beginning to get paranoid.

He began to feel that he couldn't trust the guys in Spain. Fearing that the operation may have been infiltrated, he fired some of them, which pissed off the rest. The hash business was getting to be more trouble than it was worth, so he dumped it. Dealing in heroin was a safer bet. The Turkish babas who trafficked it from Afghanistan were tough guys who seemed to be immune to infiltration by the authorities. He arranged a shipment for a mob in Liverpool in a groupage with Ecstasy, speed and cocaine which would be hidden in metal boxes attached to the sides of a haulage tanker.

But there had been a misjudgement. When Mick's courier handed over the heroin in two large sports bags, they didn't fit into the metal containers, which were already stuffed with coke, amphetamines and Ecstasy tablets. So the lorry driver had to sling the bags under his seat.

At Dover, the customs officers spotted the bags. Naturally, they wanted a look inside and found 50 kilos of heroin all neatly wrapped with duct tape which, thanks to Mick, had become our Firm's hallmark. Checking the lorry, they noticed the metal side compartments and opened them to find 7 kilos of cocaine, 50 kilos of speed and 60,000 tabs of MDMA, worth somewhere in the region of £9 million. The driver, who confessed to smuggling, got fifteen years.

Looking back, the whole operation in Amsterdam was getting lax. I blame Mick's growing habit. As they say, 'Don't get high on your own supply.'

A few days later, our bureau de change in Notting Hill Gate was hit. Officers from Customs and Excise's new National Investigation Service burst in to find something near half a million quid in old notes on the table being counted. The place was closed down, with the police alleging that the operation had laundered some £100 million in illicit cash. The manager was charged. Amazingly, he was granted bail and disappeared. Tried in his absence, it was found to be not proven that he knew the money passing through his exchange was the proceeds of crime. Our share of the missing cash had long since vanished into a black hole in Dubai where I was developing new ways to launder money.

After three weeks on the high seas, Mick's container of ingots arrived at Rotterdam's Europoort. It was busier than Amsterdam, so he figured it would be safer. What's more, it was not marked for transhipment to the UK. He planned to have it taken by train to Sofia, where we had bought a winery. Coke can be dissolved in red wine which he was then going to have bottled and shipped to England. It can be dissolved in rum too. The cocaine is precipitated out by adding ammonia.

He had chosen Bulgaria because it was outside the EU so there were no regulations on the wine. Cheap wine was shipped in from India and, to further disguise the country of origin, he had fake labels printed in Egypt, making out they were fine wines. By then he'd got things sorted out with the authorities in Bulgaria, and actually stayed in the local mayor's house when conducting business there.

The problem with his plan was that the shippers in Venezuela hadn't paid for the onward transportation of the ingots to Bulgaria, so the container was stuck in the customs compound in Rotterdam. Mick didn't want to get involved in case customs had spotted something was up with the shipment. But using coke makes you overwrought, overstrung and, worse, overconfident. Eventually, he got so frustrated that he sent a fax to the port authorities. After a week there was still no movement. The fax had been a fatal mistake. The net was closing in around him and Mick was now living on borrowed time.

At five o'clock one morning, ten paramilitary officers burst into Mick's villa in Warmond. Mick was upstairs in his bedroom, alone and unarmed. He was awoken by a stun grenade. He opened his eyes to find he was surrounded by figures in black and a gun stuck in his face. With his hands cuffed behind his back, he was taken away in an armoured car. Plainly, the

Dutch authorities thought he was dangerous. They were right. When they searched his house, they found an arsenal which could have kept them held off for weeks if they'd attacked in daylight and he'd seen them coming. He claimed they were for his personal protection. Just as the huge stash of cocaine they found, he said, was for personal use. In this case he was probably right.

Mike, who was also in the house and made similar protestations of innocence, was led away in handcuffs too.

At the same time, the house in Waverveen was raided. The rest of his gang was rounded up and more weapons were found. They were taken down the road to the police headquarters in The Hague. Mick was taken to one of the Netherlands' 'special jails' where, deprived of coke, he had to undergo cold turkey. From then on, he was shuffled around these prisons so frequently that officers from the Met, who'd been sent over, couldn't get to see him.

Meanwhile, Dutch customs opened the container. They knew what they were doing and had the right tools to cut into the ingots. Five hundred kilos of 95 per cent pure cocaine were recovered. They had Mick's fax, so he was banged to rights.

In the garage of the house in Waverveen, another 80 kilos of heroin, 60 kilos of MDMA and 200 kilos of cannabis were found, along with four assault rifles, ammunition, hand grenades, CS gas canisters, two surface-to-air missiles, false passports and €500,000 in cash. The rest of the mob were done for too.

Two laptops were taken from Mick's house and forensic experts set about combing the hard drives for details of his financial dealings. Hopefully, they would be disappointed. There should have been no records. All dealings should go through me and the figures stored in my head. But Mick had screwed up a couple of times recently. What else might they find? A casual email? A diary date? Clearly Mick was going down. Was he going to take us down with him?

# CHAPTER TWENTY-FIVE
## THE TRIAL

Mick was uncooperative so he was kept in solitary confinement, visited occasionally by his lawyer who said that, without cocaine, he was tetchy and irritable. The only other contact Mick had was with the guards who brought him his meals and the police who tried to question him. It was a waste of effort. He said nothing.

Others in the gang had elaborate cover stories, which the Dutch interrogators tried to break. But these guys were old hands and stuck to the same story through thick and thin.

With Mick, the investigators had nothing to work with. Although we suspected that the Dutch authorities had been listening in on his phone, he had no idea how extensive the surveillance had been.

Our whole drug importation racket was now in tatters and Steve set about trying to undo the damage. Between him and me, we knew most of the contacts Mick had in each arm of the operation, but we didn't know how badly they had been compromised. They were also a bit wary of working with us again until Mick had stood trial and then at least they would get a better idea of what the authorities knew. For the moment we would all have to sit tight. But the demand for drugs was still there – it always was – so if we didn't work quickly to establish new sources of supply, someone else would take over.

Then there was the money. Some of the dealers who owed Mick money thought they could get away without paying. They were soon to be proved very wrong. Steve liked to avoid violence, if possible. He felt that he could get what he wanted by reasoning with people. If not, we still had enough brawn in The Firm to make sure that everything was settled in the appropriate way. Thankfully, nobody took any liberties.

Mick's lawyer soon discovered the extent of the evidence against him. The Dutch police had been tapping his phone calls for months. He had been sloppier than we thought. He faced two charges – trafficking drugs and being a member of a criminal organisation. Mick didn't attend the committal proceedings. There was no point, he said. He wasn't going to get bail. Even if he put up a surety of £10 million, they knew he would head for southern Spain, if not further afield.

On his way to court, Mick was blindfolded and shackled before he was loaded into a helicopter in the yard of the maximum-security prison where he was being held. From there he was flown to an army base where he was loaded into an armoured van and driven in a convoy of six black Mercedes with tinted windows to the courthouse, which was ringed with special forces troops armed with machine guns.

There were officers on the roof and more in the windows of the surrounding offices, scanning the crowds with binoculars. Everyone going into and out of the courthouse had their bags searched and had to pass through a metal detector that was flanked by more armed guards wearing goggles and face masks. The courtroom on the first floor had been sealed off for the hearing. There were more armed guards outside and inside the court.

In the Netherlands, there is no jury trial. Three examining magistrates consider the evidence presented by the chief prosecutor. Mick was not required to make a formal plea of guilty or not guilty to the drug smuggling charges. He sat beside his lawyer and an interpreter who explained things as the proceedings were going on.

The prosecutor began by adding a further charge – that of being the leader of the criminal organisation he had already been charged with being a member of. Altogether, he faced a maximum sentence of sixteen years.

Mick's lawyer immediately responded by claiming that the police raids in Holland were prompted by information obtained by the illegal phone tapping of one of the calls he had made to England. That would put the whole case into contention. The argument was that, if the original information had been obtained illegally, the raids themselves were illegal too.

When the presiding magistrate asked Mick if he had anything to say, he responded calmly. He said that it was important that the court look into where the information came from that began the investigation. This was where the rivalry between the police and customs in the UK came into play again. The police said information came from customs and claimed public immunity. But customs said it came from the police. They both claimed that the information did not come from an informant, so it must have come from a phone tap.

The court wanted time to question British officials, so Mick and his team agreed to a delay in the proceedings for further investigation into the case. With that, the proceedings against him were suspended and Mick was returned to prison.

Steve and I had decided not to go over to the Netherlands for the hearings as we didn't know whether we were implicated in any way by the taps on Mick's phone. However, I was in close contact with Mick's lawyer and his interpreter, who sent fulsome reports. After all, we were paying them. Mick was also allowed to write from jail, though his letters were read and bore the stamp of a censor.

The rest of the gang appeared in court one by one. They too complained that the investigation was illegal. The allegation was that it had been started by a fax to the Dutch authorities from a British police liaison officer. Defence counsel said that the court must first discover whether the methods the British and Dutch police had used were legal. However, from the raid on the house at Waverveen, the Dutch had material evidence against them, so the proceedings against them continued.

One of them denied knowing that there was hashish in the house, though the whole place stank of it and his glasses had been found in the room where it was stored. They weren't his glasses, he said, and a car accident some years before had deprived him of his sense of smell. Another denied knowing anything about drugs, even though packages were found under his bed. The large amounts of money that he had been found with was his own, he said, though he could not explain where it had come from.

Another denied that he had any weapons, though a gun had been found under his pillow and grenades behind his headboard. Some denied knowing Mick, though he rented the house they were staying in. One claimed he was merely guarding the property. It was a mess.

Their phones had also been tapped. Their taped conversations, they said, were entirely innocent and it was up to the prosecution to prove otherwise. They claimed they were in Holland for entirely innocent purposes. Again, it was up to the prosecution to prove that this was not true. As to being members of a criminal organisation, the evidence was all circumstantial.

One case had to be postponed because the defendant was wanted in the drug-smuggling case where the lorry was caught in Dover. The guy who had done the security depot in Slough was also wanted in the UK. Another was hiding out because he had stabbed someone in London. He claimed that the man he had stabbed had insulted his wife, and he was not hiding out from the police but from the man whom he had stabbed who might seek retribution. These guys sought to delay the cases against them for as long as possible, fearing harsher treatment by the law back in the UK.

In prison, Mick remained cool. He said the only time he lost his rag was when it was said that he had only won a game of pool because the other player let him. When a TV journalist tried to get in touch, he claimed that he had been smeared by the media and the authorities were using him as a scapegoat.

Things took a turn for the worse when his next appearance in court was delayed because, the authorities said, they had received information that there was a plot to spring him. The hearings were to be shifted to a heavily guarded military base.

A clip of Mick threatening to assassinate a rival and his family with a bomb was played. Mick complained that if the whole tape had been played and this was heard in context it was clear that he was joking. It was pure hyperbole (my word, not his). He was being stitched up and there was no way that he was getting a fair trial.

Mick's mate Mike Janson admitted to piloting private flights between Colombia and Venezuela, but denied any involvements in the cocaine shipment. No evidence concerning his activities in South America was presented. Besides, it was outside Dutch jurisdiction. So he walked. Four of the guys who had been in the house at Waverveen were given five years each. Three others were extradited to the UK to face trial there. Mick was the only one charged in connection with the cocaine shipment and his case was adjourned.

Three weeks later, it was ruled that even though the investigation had been set up due to phone taps in the UK, that didn't mean that the case could not be presented in a Dutch court. Key was the fax Mick had sent to customs in Rotterdam. This connected him to the drugs shipment independent of any information supplied by the British police and gave the Dutch authorities reasonable grounds to make the searches. Again, Mick stayed in his cell rather than attend the hearing, figuring that the verdict was a foregone conclusion.

Indeed, it was. He was found to be the head of a criminal organisation that was trafficking large quantities of cocaine, cannabis and MDMA. He got ten years. Some said he was lucky. He'd have got a much harsher sentence in the UK.

But for Mick it was not going to be a walk in the park. He was sent to a maximum security prison. He was held in a special unit, a prison within a prison that he shared with terrorists and mass murderers. Phone calls were monitored and inmates strip-searched several times a day.

While Mick's lawyers put together an appeal on the grounds that the British phone tapping was illegal, the British police deemed that the proceeds from any criminal activities would be forfeited and tried tracking down his assets. Good luck there. I had scrupulously squirrelled them away.

Everything he ostensibly owned was the property of some offshore holding company. On paper, he was practically a pauper. You'd wonder why he wasn't on the dole – except that the DSS might be trying to find him a job. The Dutch police also wanted to interview Steve and me, but we found ourselves unable to cooperate.

However, we were allowed regular phone calls. I guess the authorities allowed this because they were tapping the phone in the hope that we might give something away. Mick complained about the security that the Dutch had laid on. He had been treated as if he was a terrorist.

He also said that he was feeling better now that he had given up the coke, albeit forcibly. He was tough and reckoned he could handle a ten stretch, no problem.

# CHAPTER TWENTY-SIX
## MANSLAUGHTER

In jail, Mick kept fit and did his best to learn Dutch so that he could read the court papers. This was hard for him as he wasn't a great reader, but being off the coke helped. His appeal failed, but that had been expected. Otherwise, he was popular among the other prisoners. Most of them seemed to have accepted their fate. He had not. He had a family taking care of his interests and was looking forward to living the good life when he came out.

Despite further busts, Steve and I managed to keep the supply chain of drugs going. Even a DEA-led raid on cocaine production facilities around Cali did not dent the trade too badly. There were more casualties too. Not just from shootings. One guy's kid took a couple of swigs from a bottle of rum which cocaine had been suspended in and died of an overdose.

Meanwhile for Mick, there was a setback. In the exercise yard, he was attacked by a Kurdish psychopath who was in for murder. According to Mick, while they'd been watching football on the TV that afternoon, the other prisoners had wound the psycho up. Mick had befriended him and tried to calm him down. But the guy hit him. So Mick hit him back. The guy fell, hitting his head on the floor. But he would not stay down. So Mick hit him again and kicked him several times in the head. Mick said it was self-defence.

The prisoners there were judged to be so dangerous that the guards were not allowed to intervene in a fight until they had backup. By the time they did, the guy was unconscious. He died in hospital the following day.

Mick was banished to solitary confinement while the police made their enquiries. The prison itself was a former concentration camp, so you can imagine the conditions in solitary. When the chaplain complained of the harsh treatment being meted out, he was dismissed.

Prisoners in solitary were woken every two hours at night to keep them disoriented, and phone calls and prison visits were unreasonably restricted. Some prisoners had been driven crazy by their treatment. The European Committee for the Prevention of Torture had described the conditions there as inhumane and the governor had been transferred after it had been found to be too severe. But Mick was a tough nut.

He was scheduled to appear before the examining magistrate twenty minutes away by road. But then it was deemed that, on his own, Mick might make a break for it. So a courtroom was set up in the prison and the examining magistrate came to him. The proceedings dragged on for months.

Eventually, Mick was summoned to appear at another court, where, again, security had been ramped up. But he refused to go. He was being forced to wear a bulletproof vest for the trip, as well as a hood and handcuffs, and he objected to this, saying this would prejudice the hearing as it would make him look like a dangerous criminal.

His lawyer made this case to the court, which adjourned while an attempt was made to resolve the problem. When no solution was found, the hearing resumed, but the court had deaf ears when it came to the argument that the dead man had a history of violence and that Mick had been in fear of his life. In his absence, he was convicted of manslaughter for 'having used excessive violence'. He got another three years.

Meanwhile, the Dutch Supreme Court dismissed the argument that Mick had not had a fair trial because the British officials involved in the inquiry had not appeared in court, citing diplomatic immunity, depriving the defence of the opportunity to cross-examine them. Appeal denied, though he was moved to another prison with a softer regime.

The Dutch courts also decided to go about seizing his assets. Initially, they had no more luck than the British authorities. However, they cooked up the figure of £20 million under stringent new laws that aimed to strip convicted criminals of their ill-gotten gains. Mick contested the figure, which was reduced to £5 million, then to £2 million, though interest was rapidly accruing. When he was threatened with another four years in jail for non-payment, we stumped up the money and, despite rumours that he had been drug dealing from his prison cell, he was released on parole.

# CHAPTER TWENTY-SEVEN
## THE HOMECOMING

When Mick came home we gave him a huge party in the Hippodrome, which we took over for the night. Everyone from the old neighbourhood was there. Even those that had moved away came back for the occasion. The police had a field day, waiting outside and making a note of who went in and out.

They may have been expecting trouble and nearly got some when we had an unexpected gatecrasher. Voytek had heard about the bash and was determined to steal the show. He turned up with a couple of heavies. Mick went mental. It took three of us to hold him down. Steve intervened. There was a lot of finger pointing and cursing. The peace that he had carefully brokered with the Poles over the last few years went up in smoke when Steve lost his rag and smacked Voytek one.

I thought the whole thing was going to kick off, but Voytek's minders decided that this was not the place to settle old scores. Rather too public, perhaps. As they bundled him towards the door, Voytek pointed at Mick, who, eyes blazing, was struggling to get free.

'You're not going to be able to hide behind him forever,'

Voytek told Steve. 'He's going down again. It's only a matter of time.'

Then he made a lunge at Mick, but his bruisers restrained him.

Pointing at Steve, Voytek spat: 'I'm going to have you.'

Then it was my turn. He jabbed his finger at me and said: 'As for you, punk . . .'

But by then his boys had shoved him down the stairs and out of the door.

After things had calmed down, we laughed it off and Mick spent the rest of the evening distributing largesse. Anyone who had a problem that could be fixed with a handful of cash got it. No one from the old crowd who had a dodgy deal that needed funding went away empty-handed. For a week or so afterwards, Mick drove around Notting Hill and The Town splashing the cash. He paid for a funeral, a private operation and some care home bills.

We told Mick that his Robin Hood routine was all very well, but he needed to be a bit careful. The authorities would be wanting to know where the money was coming from and his generous handouts might draw their attention to us.

If he couldn't occupy himself being a one-man charity organisation, Mick argued, he would have to go back to work. That too was impossible with the surveillance he was under. The first time he stepped out of line he would find himself back in chokey. He didn't have to worry. We would pay his living expenses, but there was to be no flash cars or high living. If he was a good boy, or appeared to be, eventually the Old Bill would get bored and leave him alone.

This was not Mick's style. He flew out to Jersey to see an old girlfriend who had moved out to the Channel Islands to work in the offshore financial industry. Almost immediately, he lumped up with his old mate Mike Janson, who turned up out of the blue. He pointed out that, on the island, drugs cost about three times what they fetched on the mainland. It was too good an opportunity to miss. Or so Mick thought.

Mick had learned his lesson from the phone taps on his mobile in Holland, so conducted all his business from phone boxes. Remember them? But he had underestimated how much the Old Bill wanted to nick him. Apparently, they felt they'd been upstaged by the Dutch police. But there were only a limited number of phone boxes within easy reach of Mick's girlfriend's flat. As Plod were keeping an eye on him 24/7, they must have spotted his frequent use of phone boxes and figured he was up to something. We learned later that they had simply bugged the ones he used most frequently. The laws on phone tapping on Jersey are somewhat laxer than those on the mainland.

The plan was for Mick and Mike to take the car ferry over to St Malo, then drive to Amsterdam to buy the drugs. They had already recruited a couple of guys with a boat to collect the shipment from the French coast and bring them to St Catherine's Breakwater at the east end of the island, so they didn't have to bring them back on the ferry.

The deal never came off. Mick only had the pocket money we were giving him and the dealers in Amsterdam couldn't be bothered to deal in such small amounts. His line of credit had run out. The vendors reckoned that, since he had been to jail once, he might end up there again and they wouldn't get their money back. It was simply not worth the risk dealing with him. Mike stayed on in Amsterdam, while Mick flew back to Jersey alone. Later he was spotted near our patch in West London, the significance of which I did not see at the time.

The fact that the drug deal hadn't come off made no difference to the Old Bill. They figured they had enough evidence from phone-box taps to get him on a charge of conspiracy to import drugs. It also appeared that swift-footed Plod had managed to bug the car they used to drive from St Malo to Amsterdam, chatting about the drugs deal along the way.

A few days after Mick got back to Jersey, he was walking down the seafront at St Helier with his girlfriend when three unmarked cars came screeching to a halt. Plain-clothed policemen jumped out, manhandled him to the ground and cuffed him. They took him to La Moye prison.

He languished there behind razor wire and CCTV cameras

for over a year before he came to trial. We figured that it wouldn't be a good idea if Steve was seen in court, but I risked it. Although I had two brothers who were known gangsters dealing in coke, as far as the police were concerned, I was still Snow White, if you'll pardon the pun.

The police on Jersey were not to be outdone by the Dutch police. They borrowed an armoured prison van from the Met to transport Mick the eight miles from La Moye to the Royal Court in St Helier, which was surrounded by every armed cop on the island.

The Jersey Police offered Mick a deal. If he pleaded guilty, he'd get just eight years with no confiscation of assets. That didn't bother him too much as neither the Dutch nor the British police had managed to find out where his money had gone.

Mick turned down the deal and the trial went ahead. His defence was that the Plod had fitted him up. Indeed, the evidence from the bug in the car was ruled inadmissible and the judge gave the police a slap on the wrist as they had no authority to collect evidence by means of a bug in France, Belgium or the Netherlands, the countries Mick and Mike had travelled through in the rental car. However, the evidence from the bugged phone boxes was enough. Mick got twelve years and was sent to HMP Whitemoor in Cambridgeshire, not so far that I couldn't visit. I was always surprised to find how chipper he was. Clearly, he liked the company of other criminals. It would have depressed the hell out of me. But then he didn't have a wife and kids on the outside that would be missing him.

The police had still not been able to find any money, so the courts hit him with a confiscation order, threatening him with another ten years if he did not pay up. For Mick, this was a matter of pride. He appealed and lost, so stayed on in jail. Maybe it wasn't just pride. It was discovered later that he was banging one of the teachers who visited the prison to help with inmates' rehabilitation. A prison warder walked in to find her bent over a desk with her skirt around her waist and Mick behind her. She was dismissed.

And it didn't end there. It was found out that one of the prison guards had been persuaded to strip off for sexy snaps, which she smuggled into the jail. When Mick praised her figure, things went further and she began smuggling mobile phones and cocaine into Whitemoor. She was jailed herself.

Now with several black marks on his record, Mick was transferred to the maximum-security prison at Belmarsh, which nestles behind Woolwich Crown Court. This was far more convenient for me to visit when I was still living in London.

At Belmarsh, Mick was consigned to the SSU – the Special Secure Unit which is basically a top-security prison within a top-security prison. It housed some of the most dangerous prisoners in the country. Not that Mick is particularly dangerous, without a shooter at least. He had just been a bad boy. Not only had he got away with having sex, drugs and mobile phones in jail, he had also intimidated prison officers. He scared one guard shitless when Mick asked how his wife's dental appointment had gone. Somehow he had found out that she was having her wisdom teeth extracted. Little things like that, which were more than likely just picked up on the prison grapevine, can put the wind up the warders and put you under close surveillance.

In the SSU, every move Mick made was watched and noted down in his blue Category A book. This book went with him everywhere he went. Mick told me that if he had to go anywhere off his own spur of cells in House Block 4, he had to be accompanied by at least three prison staff: one to carry his Category A book, one to watch him closely and one who kept a fierce Alsatian on a short leash. You only had to make a sudden move before all hell broke loose.

The high-security prisoners there are under observation at all times and no one has ever escaped from Belmarsh. The prison wall is 25 feet tall with an anti-grapple dome covering the top of the outer wall. That made it impossible to scale the wall, because if you threw up a grappling hook, or any type of hook, it couldn't get a grip on the smooth sides of the dome.

Inside the perimeter wall, there are 20-foot fences made

from green high-tension wire, topped with coils of razor wire that would tear you to shreds if you tried to get over it. Everywhere, inside and out, there are CCTV cameras.

The steel doors are on swing hinges. This means they could open either way, so you can't barricade them. Mick told me that the small windows in the cell have bars made of manganese that can't be cut and a steel grille. The place is a bloody fortress.

To visit, you go to reception on Belmarsh Way. Once you've handed over any bag you're carrying, then been through the metal detector, you're patted down. After that, you're put in a windowless van and driven around a bit before reaching the visitors' area. This, apparently, is so that you lose your bearings. You won't have seen any landmarks on the way, nor will you even know the direction you've come from. So if anyone is planning an escape, the visitor could impart no useful information.

Mick told me that there were seventy prisoners on his spur, under constant surveillance, with CCTV cameras on every landing. The cells themselves were modern and spartan. There was a metal-framed bed bolted to the floor, an MDF cupboard bolted to the wall, a chair and a toilet. The visitors' area itself was clean and bright, very different from Pentonville and the Scrubs where I used to visit Dad. Still, it was not a place that I wanted to end up in either.

Naturally, Mick made the best of it. I don't know how he did it, but he still managed to get drugs and mobile phones in there and carried on business as usual. I guess as there was no chance that anyone could escape, the screws could not be bothered what they got up to inside.

But still it gave me the willies. Short of anything else to charge me with, the police could always accuse me of smuggling the phone and drugs in to him.

# ACT IV

## GANG WARS

### 2012–20

# CHAPTER TWENTY-EIGHT
## ESCAPE TO THE COUNTRY

Steve was now a family man and wanted to get out of town where his kids could breathe some fresh air. He found an old manor house in the Kent countryside near Dartford. It was an area where a lot of the old mobsters went to retire. Nearby Erith was considered the heart of 'sawn-off-shotgun territory' because of the number of armed robbers that had come from that area.

But Steve was in no mood for putting his feet up, or shuffling around one of the nearby golf courses reminiscing about the old times. With Mick now firmly banged up and out of the game, he was busier than ever. But with modern encrypted communication, like so many now in the post-Covid era, he found he could work from home.

For him, Dartford was a good place to keep an eye on business. It was on a direct route to Dover and Folkestone, where some of our merchandise was coming into the country. And thanks to the Dartford Tunnel and the new Queen Elizabeth II Bridge, it was easy to get back into town, or to the container ports on the north side of the river at Thurrock and Tilbury, attracting more modern-day criminals. It was also on a direct route to Bexhill-on-Sea, so it was easy to take the kids to see their grandparents whom we were still supporting in some style.

That area of north Kent was considered England's equivalent of the Costa del Crime. Local historians say that it always had that reputation. The river there marked the border between two clan territories from the fourteenth to seventeenth centuries, so many of their equivalents of gangland wars were fought along the banks of the Thames there.

There was a rumour in Steve's local pub that the wreck of a small galleon packed with stolen gold lies so deep in the mudbank near the crossing that no one has been able to find it even at the lowest of tides. But that doesn't stop them looking.

As a literary aside, Charles Dickens' *Great Expectations* starts there when the convict Magwitch escapes from the prison hulks moored nearby. The opening scene of *Our Mutual Friend* refers to a man who makes his living fishing dead bodies out of the Thames in the vicinity. Corpses floating downstream now wash up on the muddy shores of Greenhithe. Dickens also wrote about young women being taken across the river there to work in the workhouses and brothels of East London, just as people traffickers do today.

Brian Reader was arrested in Dartford after masterminding the break-in at the vaults in Hatton Garden. Kenny Noye had lived out there too. Then when the gang that tried to steal half a million quids' worth of diamonds from the Millennium Dome had another go, they rammed a security van in Aylesford in Kent.

Just the other side of the river, the Essex Boys came to public attention after the death of schoolgirl Leah Betts, who took a tab of Ecstasy on her eighteenth birthday and fell into a coma. Four days later she was pronounced dead and her life support system was turned off. The Ecstasy had been supplied by the Essex Boys. Three weeks later, three leading members of the gang were found dead in a Range Rover parked in a dirty track near Rettendon in Essex while awaiting drugs being flown in on a small plane. They had each been killed by a shotgun blast to the head.

The bloody war in Kosovo brought other criminals, who saw the UK as rich pickings and settled in the area. They were followed by Albanians who pretended to be refugees from Kosovo. Russian mafiosi, largely from Vladimir Putin's home town of St Petersburg, attached themselves to a number of billionaire oligarchs who had decided to move to England and came over with them. In London, they could launder money easily and if anything went wrong they would be just a short distance from the Channel ports to make their escape.

While British criminals had largely given up armed robbery after the failure of the Millennium Dome diamond heist, the Eastern Europeans persisted. The Albanian gangsters tried their hand at what became the biggest cash robbery in UK history when they took £53 million from the Securitas depot in Tonbridge, Kent, leaving another £154 million because they did not have the means to transport it. The Eastern Europeans only employed local criminals as accomplices because they believed that it was necessary to keep the British underworld onside if they were going to pull off such a daring heist.

The local criminals were not happy with the Albanians. They had been told that guns would only be used to threaten the staff at the Tonbridge depository. Later they discovered that two of the Albanians had fought in the Balkans and were hardened killers who wouldn't hesitate to shoot. What's more, the depot manager and his family were to be kidnapped at gunpoint. If something went wrong, they would all be going down for much longer sentences. Indeed, they did.

The warehouse where the heist was planned was near the Dartford Crossing. In the end, the British and Albanian criminals fell out over the split of the cash that brought about their capture. The thieves were quickly rounded up and got from eighteen years to life. It would be the end of any further cooperative ventures and soured the relations between the locals and Eastern Europeans in the area.

Romanians who had moved into the area soon made their

own approach to the Colombian cartels and began undercutting us. Meanwhile, the Albanians were growing their own cannabis plants and producing their own hash in the mountains around Tirana.

The old-style British criminals resented the fact that the newcomers didn't even bother to learn English. This led the foreign gangs to get together. They realised that controlling the Dartford Crossing was vital. Key to this was the territory between Dartford, Swanley and West Kingsdown, three towns that had been home to professional criminals for fifty years. The area was known to the locals as The Bermuda Triangle – what went in rarely came out again.

This little patch of the Garden of England basically ran on a criminal economy and, as all the dyed-in-the-wool gangsters knew each other, it operated as a criminal intelligence network. Clearly, if the Eastern Europeans could establish a foothold there in Kent, they could move on to Essex, London and beyond.

It seemed that Steve had jumped from the frying pan into the fire. Once the new wave of foreign criminals dominated the Dartford Crossing, our hard-won West London manor would be in their sights. Instead of enjoying the peace of the countryside, Steve was on the front line and the battle was about to begin.

There was a third party in this conflict, of course – the

police. They had a control tower overlooking the southern exit of the crossing so they could monitor the traffic coming southbound over the bridge. But we could hardly depend on the police to be on our side. They just weren't that patriotic.

Things began to change when Vladimir Putin was standing for re-election in 2012 – this was back in the day when Russian elections weren't routinely fixed and when he had wanted to show the people that he had a clean pair of hands. Members of the St Petersburg Mafia who had followed the oligarchs to London began disappearing. That was no skin off our nose. In fact, it rid us of what may have become dangerous rivals.

But on this, we were a little over-optimistic. As the numbers of the Russian Mafia were depleted, along with some of the oligarchs who died in increasingly mysterious ways, criminal gangs from Eastern Europe got the idea that the UK was open house. At first they brought weapons, largely from the decommissioned security forces in their countries. Then they went to people smuggling and trafficking young women for prostitution. This was something we didn't do (it crossed a line for us), so they were no direct competition. We may be criminals, but we have standards. However, the trucks that brought the illegal immigrants from the Channel ports came directly through Kent and across the Dartford Crossing, so that was where the foreign criminals set up their headquarters.

Of course, some of the older British gangsters who lived there objected to this invasion of their patch and encouraged the younger generation to strike back. Unfortunately, that was not so easy. The Eastern Europeans had much more firepower.

There were murders. Not only did the Eastern Europeans pick a fight with the Brits, they also fought among themselves and a brutal turf war broke out. A Ukrainian gang turned up and tried to buy up land in the area to launder dirty money. Flashing cash around attracted the police. The Albanians didn't take to them either. Some were killed. The others fled back to Odessa. The Ukrainians hadn't realised that it was the Eastern Europeans that controlled the area, not the British.

The British criminals had another disadvantage. The Eastern European gangs were impossible to infiltrate by undercover cops. They knew each other from back home, so it was easy to spot any interloper. A British copper is not going to be able to pass himself off as a street urchin from Kharkiv. And due to the language difference, it was also difficult for Plod to get any intelligence on them, even if they got within earshot. Tap their mobiles? Intercept their texts? Scotland Yard doesn't have that many translators, whereas our British guys could give away some vital information, completely innocently, simply by being overheard chatting in a pub.

Once the Eastern Europeans got into drugs, they found

some of their British rivals easy pickings. If the Brits were buying their cocaine through the usual routes, it would have been cut at every stage along the way. By the time it got to the user in the UK, there would be practically no active ingredient in it. That meant that the buyer would not come back for more.

We had maintained our contacts in Cali, so what was shipped was 99 per cent pure. The only cutting done was by us when it got here. Steve made sure that the cocaine content remained high, which helps with repeat purchases. Sure, it was cut again when we passed it on down the distribution chain, but the dealers were warned to give value for money or they would find themselves out of business. The heroin trade worked the same way. I know it sounds unethical, but you have to get the user hooked. Otherwise their custom simply fades away.

At street level, there were run-ins between the local criminals and those from Eastern Europe and then a fresh influx from Latvia. Guns were used and there were fatal stabbings. This was under-reported in the British media as it was eclipsed by the epidemic of knife crime that was going on nationwide anyway.

Now, as he was growing older, Steve liked to avoid confrontations when he could. He sought to come to an accommodation with the newcomers, figuring that there was enough business to go round for all of us. He admired the organisational skills of the Eastern European gangs, particularly the younger members who performed incredible stunts on their motor scooters practising for the sort of smash-and-grab jobs on high-end West End shops that he and Mick used to pull off when they were young.

The youngsters hit the jewellery shops of Bond Street and Hatton Garden, the designer clothes shops of the West End and the City, and the electronic stores of Tottenham Court Road. The loot would then be brought back across the river, then on across the Channel. The Eastern Europeans had a ready market for luxury goods as their homelands benefited from accession to the EU. Nobody there was worried if a Bulgari watch or a Stella McCartney frock was nicked. Who was going to know?

The young gangsters were also trained to start up any scooter without a key in seconds. A couple of them nicked an Aprilia SR GT and hit an electrical shop in Central London at one in the morning. Producing a sledgehammer from the back of the bike, they smashed their way into the store and fled with over £200,000 of electronic equipment. The alarm bells rang, but the robbers were off before anyone could respond. The whole thing was caught on CCTV, but their features were hidden by full-face crash helmets. Job done. It was happening all the time.

Some of the older British criminals disapproved of the way the foreigners used boys as young as sixteen as foot soldiers and paid them as little as possible. It was so bad that one of the scooter gangs was even dubbed Fagin's Kitchen Crew. It seems that I wasn't the only one who read Dickens.

The foreign gangs were workaholics too. Some would drive from Sofia to North London in one day carrying drugs. Nor were they users. British criminals like to booze and snort the stuff themselves. Apart from the odd glass of champagne, Steve didn't lose himself in any vices. I drank wine, but I didn't do the white stuff. It's been the undoing of so many in our business. Mick was the only one who did it, but largely, I think, to pass the time in jail.

To build a bridge with other crime bosses, Steve also changed his image. Giving up the flash cars associated with wealthy drug barons, he bought a London taxi and had it converted into a mobile office and communications centre. It also boasted a state-of-the-art television. He could conduct business on the hoof, if needs be.

The Eastern European bosses used similarly downmarket accommodation. They ran their businesses out of converted shipping containers. These had the advantage that they could easily be moved around to stay one step ahead of the cops. They were also suitably anonymous. You could not easily tell one from any of the hundreds scattered around the area.

Containers were also used to house the younger gangsters. Otherwise, they were made to sleep two to a bed in some shit-hole property down by the river. They were treated like dirt. Their bosses hardly seemed to care if they lived or died. We never treated our crew that way. It would hardly inspire loyalty. Our guys were largely locals from our old neighbourhood, or their family and friends. You had to know whom to trust.

And they were mainly men. We only used women for specific tasks, such as drug or money mules, as the authorities seemed to be less suspicious or give them an easier ride. Organised crime is not an equal opportunity employer, as I'm sure you can see from the prison occupancy stats.

The other business the Eastern Europeans came to dominate was nicking cars. They would nick top-of-the-range BMWs, Mercs and Porsches in town. The cars had to be worth at least £100,000 for it to be worthwhile. Target vehicles were often surreptitiously fitted with a tracking device by the gangs so they could pick the perfect moment to pounce in a remote location away from prying CCTV cameras.

All cars crossing the Queen Elizabeth II Bridge are monitored electronically, but south of the river they would be taken to a lorry park where a mechanic would be waiting to change the licence plates as quick as pit crew change the tyres on a Formula One car at a Grand Prix. A wad of cash would then change hands. Then it was a relatively short drive to the

Channel ports for shipment onwards to be sold on the Continent. Otherwise, they would be taken to Tilbury or Harwich for shipping on to North Cyprus or the Middle East where there was a huge market for prestige cars. Upmarket motors were even being stolen to order.

Albanian gangs often employed Kosovans as carjackers. They were great drivers and reputed to be madmen. In one case, a businessman had stopped at a traffic light in his fancy sports car, only to be dragged out at gunpoint. The gunman then jumped in and drove away. The next time the car was seen it was on the road in Riga or Riyadh.

Steve got to know some of the foreign bosses quite well. When they had first come over, they had been prepared to work with the local criminals, but relations soon soured as the Brits by and large hated foreigners and treated them like shit. Steve was smart enough to know that that was no way to do business and always treated everyone with respect.

But there was always trouble with other local criminals who didn't like foreigners muscling in on their patch. Steve had no problem because we never operated in that manor. Although he had moved down there to live in the countryside, our business was based in West London, not Kent or Essex.

Locals who kicked up a fuss soon found they had bitten off more than they could chew. One British gang tried to ambush a bunch of Albanians one night in the darkened streets of a trading estate under the bridge. The response was swift and brutal. Two of the Brits 'went for a swim' and were never seen again. Caught on an ebbing tide, bodies quickly found themselves in the middle of the North Sea.

As the only one talking to both sides, Steve tried to keep the peace, but it was a hopeless task. Eastern European gangs from Essex and Kent joined forces to take the fight to the British gangsters on their very doorstep. The Brits had long considered the shopping centres at Lakeside in Essex and Bluewater in Kent as safe havens. They took their families there to shop, go to the cinema and eat out. These territories were off limits. Eastern Europeans displayed no such sensitivities. Jewellery stores there were targeted by a Romanian gang who torched cars in access roads to impede the police. It was their calling card. Stores there were attacked repeatedly, showing that the foreign gangs meant business. The local criminals got the message and kept their families at home, but the old boys grumbled and planned their revenge.

What made it worse was that some of the younger Albanians were particularly cocky with it all. They posted pictures on social media showing them with Bentleys, Ferraris and scantily clad girls, flashing Rolexes and waving wads of £50 notes. They even released a rap video stuffed full of bling. One clip showed them surrounding a cop car taunting the police. The older Albanians and established gang bosses weren't happy with this as they had made an effort to stay under the radar.

The younger guys were not so much of a bother as they competed largely with the 'top boy' street dealers who controlled the local housing estates. Otherwise, when the Brits pushed back against the crime bosses, the older Albanians had a secret weapon – a hitman named The Warrior. His weapon of choice was a bomb, which he used to disguise a hit as a terror attack. That kept the younger generation in order, for the moment.

Meanwhile, Steve tried to broker broader peace where he could. After all, the old-style Brits, though disgruntled, were no real threat to the newcomers and there was no point in killing just for the sake of it. For a while, the bloodshed stopped, though the ceasefire was fragile. With new competing gangs of Eastern Europeans coming in, everyone began preparing for war.

# CHAPTER TWENTY-NINE
## INTERNATIONAL RELATIONS

In league with the Turks, the Albanians tied up the heroin trade in Kent and Essex. They also took over the brothels which, again, was not a business we were into. Nevertheless, it made sense for us to form an alliance with the Albanians. They had got permission from the 'Ndrangheta in Calabria to deal directly with the Colombians after the cartels had fallen out with the Poles who had tried to muscle in. So they were getting cocaine for £5,000 a kilo in South America, rather than £22,500 a kilo in Amsterdam. As this was the same deal we were getting, it made sense to share shipping costs and smuggling routes that now focused on Tilbury and Harwich, which had good connections to Amsterdam and Rotterdam and were conveniently just over the river from Dartford. We were also dealing with the Turks for heroin as they controlled the easterly routes.

Our competition now was the new generation of Polish criminals who were coming over. They joined a community of nearly a million Poles, mostly in West London, the legacy of World War II. Many Poles had come to fight for the British when Germany and the Soviet Union invaded in 1939. At the end of the war in 1945, Poland was occupied by the Soviets, so many Poles did not dare return. They were allowed to resettle in the UK. Among them were the parents of Voytek and the other Poles at my school. Since the accession of Poland to the EU in 2004, many thousands more arrived.

In comparison, the Albanians and Turks only numbered in their thousands, so it made sense for them to join up with the distribution network we had already established. We also had the funds to finance the business. As many of the Albanians had come over on dodgy passports, they couldn't set up legitimate businesses to launder the money. We had already established front companies. We also knew how the bureaucracy worked and what the taxman would be looking out for. In return for our expertise, the Albanians would help stop the Poles moving in on our protection rackets. Because of their numbers, Polish gangsters had a notorious reputation, but even they were not as bad as the Albanians who had served in the Balkan Wars.

One of the problems with allying ourselves with the Albanians was that most Eastern Europeans have little time for Black people. Mind you, some of the old-time British criminals were little better. As our gang was from Notting Hill, we had a number of members of Caribbean or African origin. To keep the peace, they looked after business with me in West London and did not make too many trips down to Kent to see Steve.

One useful thing about having the Eastern Europeans around was the academy. It began in the early 2000s with a bunch of international jewel thieves called the Pink Panthers. They stole millions of pounds' worth of jewellery. Their first heist was £500,000 worth of diamonds stolen from a jeweller's in London's Mayfair which were then hidden in a jar of face cream. This ploy had been seen in the film *The Return of the Pink Panther*, giving the gang their nickname. In 2013, they broke into the Carlton Hotel in Cannes and made off with $136 million worth of gems and jewellery being stored by the Leviev diamond house for an exhibit. This was thought to have been the biggest jewel robbery in history.

The members of the gang were Serbs but they had been taught their craft at the 'thieves' academy' in Bucharest. It was run by a coalition of gangs who had been using the same tactics and decided to get together to pool their talent. After a number of alumni committed heists in the UK and the academy in Romania was closed down, it was decided to open something similar here. It was set up in two shipping containers which acted as classrooms. These were taken back and forth between Kent and Essex, training a number of eager young students.

There were lessons on how to evaluate jewellery at a glance and what specialist tools to use to break in quickly and safely. Each member of a team should have a specific role and heists should be timed precisely, as Steve and Mick had in the old armed robbery days. Phones shouldn't be used on a job and cars should be avoided. It was better to use a bicycle or public transport to travel to and from a robbery. Cars were easy to identify and car chases rarely turn out well. Bicycles outpace a pursuer on foot, can go down narrow alleys and through the gaps in traffic where a car chasing them cannot follow. Then they can be easily abandoned, while in an urban transportation system it is easy to get lost among a crowd.

As the academy became more popular, classes were added on forensics, when students were taught how to avoid leaving evidence at the scene of the crime, and how to spot if you are being followed. Then there were lessons on casing a joint and mapmaking. Targets should be reconnoitred in detail with entrances and exits identified. The academy was eventually closed down after one gang of graduates were arrested in the West Midlands and blew the gaff.

Shipping containers were also converted into makeshift gyms or clubs with a bar where gangsters relaxed with girls brought over from Eastern Europe. They were open twenty-four hours a day. Again to avoid problems with the police, they were moved every few nights and once a month the outside was repainted. Their location was texted to regular customers on WhatsApp.

These clubs also doubled as brothels with small bedrooms

installed at the back. The conditions for the girls were grim, but Steve's gangster friends assured him that they were not held captive there. Although they ate, drank, slept and worked in the container, they were replaced every month by a fresh intake. The previous shift either went home or went on to work in other places. That was one story at least.

It was also said that these container brothels were used to try out girls before moving them on to bigger and more lucrative brothels in London or some other city. These were usually run by the Russian Mafia and the bedrooms were often equipped with secret cameras, for security, but also for blackmail.

Clearly sex slavery was involved in this trade and the fate of these girls can only be imagined. Horrific stories have appeared in the press. On the other hand, the girls working out of the containers were well protected. If any of their customers abused them, they would suffer dire consequences. The body of an abuser would be dumped in the Thames Estuary when the tide was going out. Their passport and papers would be burned. If they were in a truck or had a vehicle, it would be resprayed, the plates changed and it would be sold on.

This was another business we didn't want to get into. Nor did other British gangsters. Most thought that pimps were the lowest of the low.

Okay, perhaps we should not be too moralistic as most of

our money came from the sale of drugs. But no one was forced to use the cocaine, weed or heroin we supplied. Even if they got hooked they knew what they were getting into, and you could always get off them if you wanted to. The NHS provided rehab centres for free.

Polish gangs also trafficked older women to work as cleaners or maids, or to be put to work in illegal factories. In many cases these women came voluntarily because they thought that they would have a better life in the UK. Some women even came to run mini brothels out of Airbnbs. They were often the widows of famous gangsters back home and so commanded respect. Others used their dead husband's connections to work high up in the drugs trade so that they could continue living the luxurious lifestyle they'd become accustomed to.

# CHAPTER THIRTY
## THE WASHING MACHINE

I was worried that Steve was getting too close to his Eastern European neighbours. They had a chilling reputation for extreme violence, often resorting to brutal torture if they thought it was necessary. Some, I guess, even did it for fun.

Besides, they seemed determined to take over the whole of the drugs trade in the UK. That meant we were a rival and would, sooner or later, be pushed out of the business – perhaps not in a very pleasant way. We still had some clout because of the reputation of our banged-up brother, whom they were now calling Mad Mickey. But that would not last forever as there was no prospect of him getting out soon. Then again we were not as young as we had once been, and there would always be an up-and-coming Young Turk ready to depose the older generation.

Discretion being the better part of valour, I suggested that we gave way, gave up drug smuggling and stuck to the one sphere of criminality that we could conduct without treading on anyone's toes – the lucrative business of money laundering. It was something that we – that is, I – had become expert in. We had a solid reputation in the underworld and knew enough big-time crooks who would pay well for our services. Even the Eastern Europeans would use us because they trusted us with their money more than they trusted each other.

One of the ways I was laundering money was dealing in property. This meant mixing with the rich and famous, who often dislike paying taxes so were keen to use our cleaning services. Steve and I were invited to posh parties, receptions and race meetings. There was still something chic about being seen in the company of gangsters, especially gangsters who dressed well. Vittoria and Steve's wife loved it, dressing to the nines for an appearance at Wimbledon or Ascot. For the latter at least, the morning suit did get a second outing.

Despite the occasional appearance in the background of a picture in the society pages, we still had to keep a low profile. We could not be seen to be flaunting our wealth with yachts, Lamborghinis, villas on the Côte d'Azur or private jets. That would attract the attention of HMRC or even the Serious Fraud Squad. We had to be ever present but invisible – more like discreet house guests than posh club members. We had neither the education nor the breeding for that. We were still really just a couple of boys from The Town. We knew our place.

It seems that we were getting out of the drugs business just in time. The last big British-run operation in the Dartford area was the gang led by the Hanna brothers, Cavan and Jamie. The Albanians got rid of them by the simple expedient of grassing them up. They had been selling Ecstasy and amphetamines. When the police swooped, they caught the brothers counting £1 million in cash.

Their drugs factory contained an industrial mixing machine, Ecstasy tablets with an estimated street value of £60,000 and 83 kilos of amphetamines worth around £828,000. The police also found notebooks that the brothers used to record their drug-dealing transactions. They showed that in just three months alone they made £38 million. They are thought to have had up to £6.1 million in assets in Britain with more overseas.

Pleading guilty to supplying Class A drugs and money laundering, they got fourteen years. Released on licence, they went right back into business. This time they were caught by the use of technology. Like a lot of criminals at the time, they had been using EncroChat, an end-to-end encrypted service that was supposedly secure favoured by criminals.

The phones they used were usually modified Android devices with the GPS, camera and microphone functions turned off, so the owner couldn't be tracked or spied on. They were sold with EncroChat pre-installed.

Devices with EncroChat could be booted in two modes. When only the power button was pressed to turn the handset on, the phone booted to a dummy Android home screen. But when the handset was switched on by pressing the power button together with the volume button, the phone booted to a secret, encrypted partition for secret communication via EncroChat's servers in France. There was also a PIN that erased all data on the phone, so you could delete all the evidence if you got caught.

EncroChat phones were expensive – around £900 for the handset and £1,350 for a six-month contract to use the service – but most gangsters thought they were worth it. They were wrong. The French Gendarmerie had cracked the system, installing malware that allowed them to read texts before they were sent. The messages were then shared with other law enforcement agencies, including Britain's National Crime Agency who argued that this was not illicit phone tapping as the texts were read from the phone not during transmission. It's a moot point. The jury's still out on that one.

The French also managed to disable the wipe function. So when Plod swooped on the Hanna brothers a second time, they seized their encrypted phones, which showed that they were shipping 89 kilos of cocaine worth £3.5 million across the country. High-end watches and cocaine were found in Cavan's home. Jamie, having not learned his lesson from the first time they were caught, was found with notes recording their drug deals. A jury convicted them of conspiracy to supply Class A drugs and conspiracy to transfer criminal property. They got twenty-five years.

Instead of EncroChat, we used PGP – Pretty Good Privacy, another program used for encrypting and decrypting emails and texts. So far it hasn't been broken, but the police can force you to give up your passwords and keys under the Regulation of Investigatory Powers Act. You can be jailed if you refuse, but it has not come to that yet.

Even though we intended to get out of the drugs business, with the influx of Eastern Europeans, life in the underworld was getting more dangerous. Steve reckoned that we should up our armour. He took me to a specialist arms supplier. To my surprise, she was a woman who had once been in the police force. Her story was that she had been booted out of the Met after supplying a South London gangster with a shooter. Her excuse was that she was trying to recruit him as an informant. It didn't wash and she had to go.

Although she had been around long before the Eastern Europeans had arrived, they wanted to put her out of business on the grounds that, as an ex-cop, she must be a grass. But she was a tough nut. The Albanians kidnapped her and threatened to kill her if she didn't hand over her business. She refused, standing up to everything they threw at her. After all, without her they did not have a business. Eventually, she earned their grudging respect. However, the locals told a different story. They said she was just a front man, or front woman, for the Eastern Europeans, who had taken over the business on the QT. They certainly gave her protection when she fell out with a gang from North London, and they were also her best customers.

Like the Eastern Europeans, she worked out of a container. It sat sometimes in the garden of her house on the outskirts of Dartford, although it was moved around the various properties she owned in the area. Again the location any given day was posted to potential customers on WhatsApp.

The place was an Aladdin's cave of an armoury. Guns of all kinds hung from the walls. An armed robber's wet dream. She even did short-term rentals. Eastern European lads would pick up a gun on the way to do a job in town and drop it off on the way to the Channel ports on their way back. Everyone paid in cash, of course.

At the time, she was selling Czech Skorpion machine pistols. Apparently the first batch she'd got her hands on were supplied by British soldiers who had picked them up in the Balkans, presumably nicked from the bodies of dead Serbs. In Eastern Europe, it was the must-have weapon for mobsters and so Skorpions were much in demand.

Naturally, Steve wanted to try one out. The gun shop hostess took us to a two-acre field in the countryside at which she kept an illicit firing range. It's odd. I guess I had been a fully paid-up gangster for decades by then, but it was the first time I had handled a firearm. I'd always left that to Steve and, more especially, Mick. Loosing off a few rounds felt surprisingly good. With the stock folded, the Skorpion could be fired one-handed and was extremely effective for robberies and assassinations, I was told.

It has to be said that our lady was a bit circumspect with us. She preferred dealing with the Eastern Europeans as they showed her more respect than the British usually did. They didn't drink or take drugs and knew what they wanted and paid up. British old-timers moaned all the time about how much better it was before the foreigners turned up. They were picky and tight-fisted, she said.

It was also safer working with the Eastern Europeans. British gangs could easily be infiltrated whereas the Eastern Europeans were practically untouchable. Plus, the Brits thought she should be grateful because they supported her after she got chucked out of the Met.

Once we got talking about it, she said that, if they liked, Brits could try buying guns off other home-grown arms smugglers. Unfortunately, they had a pretty poor record (probably grassed up by the Eastern Europeans, who knew the sources they were coming from on the Continent as these were usually their brothers in arms in the former Soviet Bloc). After our chat, we paid up, took our guns and left.

As the tension increased, we were not the only ones getting tooled up. Now the Eastern Europeans had gone into armed robbery, the province of the old-school British crims forty years before, this further racked up the resentment and they too visited our lady armourer.

One night, the old-timers struck back with a raid on a weed farm run by the Romanians in the middle of Kent. This proved to be a mistake. The Romanians had booby-trapped the place with tripwires and explosives. Two of the Brits ended up in hospital. It would've been worse but the Old Bill turned up before the Romanians could shoot the survivors.

A warning was then issued. If any of the Brits got blown up breaking in there again, the Romanians would take their bodies and dump them on the doorsteps of the other old-timers in the area. Further taking the piss, a gang of Albanian burglars broke into a number of old lags' homes, nicking hundreds of pounds' worth of their personal stuff. Others, dressed as Old Bill, stopped their cars and robbed them at gunpoint. This is what prompted Brian Reader and his bunch of old-timers to rob the security vault in Hatton Garden. It was all about recovering their self-esteem. They had once ruled the roost and wanted to show the newcomers that they still had it in them. They didn't, though.

Reader's mob had not moved with the times and on the Hatton Garden job were defeated by technology. CCTV had picked up their cars circling in the area. The police eavesdropped on their mobile phones. Their cars were bugged.

Tracking devices were fixed to them. Brian Reader even used a Freedom Pass to travel from Dartford to Hatton Garden, seemingly unaware that its use was automatically recorded, making it simply easy to track. Nor had he even disposed of the mobile phone he had used during the heist. Consequently, the gang were quickly rounded up. Even though they were given relatively short sentences of between six and seven years, two of them died of old age in prison. Perhaps they would have got away with it if they had taken some young Eastern European along with them who would have been hip to the modern world.

Even the world of money laundering we worked in was hardly safe – not if you dealt in Russian money that is. In December 2014, a supposed billionaire money launderer mysteriously fell 60 feet from the window of a £3 million apartment in Marylebone, Central London, and was impaled on the spiked railings four storeys below. He had been involved in a multimillion-pound divorce case at the time and, lo and behold, it was found he had no money. He had been involved in a £2 billion shopping and office development in Moscow, but the money seemingly disappeared into accounts in Switzerland, Monaco, the Bahamas and the British Virgin Islands.

There were other mysterious deaths among those involved in the deal, including that of the oligarch Boris Berezovsky who was found apparently hanged inside a locked bathroom in the guest suite of his former home in Berkshire. Two participants fell under the wheels of London Underground trains. One died in a helicopter crash after saying he feared for his life. Another fell to his death from the rooftop car park of Whiteleys shopping centre on Queensway, which was just at the edge of our patch.

The word was that these guys had been rubbed out by the Russian Mafia. It was said that one of them had been dangled from the balcony of a room in the Dorchester Hotel because he owed them money. Even the Albanians thought this was a bit extreme. They thought the Russians were psychos, not just because of the amount of unnecessary violence they used. The Albanians could be brutal too, torturing and mutilating those who crossed them. But they stayed below the radar. They figured that the police did not much mind if Eastern Europeans were butchering each other, but when they started doing it to Brits in such a public way, they were inviting the full force of the state to come down on them. Coming from former communist, totalitarian countries, they knew just what that meant. So the Albanians wanted to stay away from the Russians. They were money launderers, while the Albanians prided themselves on being hard-working criminals, but we could be seen as direct competition.

# CHAPTER THIRTY-ONE
## KARLO

Steve reckoned that we could take advantage of the situation with a reorganisation. Although he came up to town regularly, I pretty much ran the operation in West London. In fact, it pretty much ran itself except for an ongoing turf war with Voytek and the Poles. The young recruits he'd brought in from Poland were eager to have a go and since our confrontation at the Hippodrome he was starting to throw his weight around. It was hard to hold the line, but we still had some trusted lieutenants.

With me in charge in West London, Steve would now confine his operations to Kent and the south-east. He had got chummy with the clan chief of the Albanians in Dartford whom we will call Karlo. Not just chummy. Steve's son was now nineteen and had knocked up Karlo's teenage daughter, but the Albanian hard man liked the boy and insisted that they get married. The wedding was a fine thing. Karlo had run up a makeshift ballroom for the reception. It was a fine sight to see all the Albanian crooks bunched up at one end and Steve's old-time British gangster friends at the other, eyeing each other suspiciously.

Now that we were all family, Steve suggested that we formalise our arrangement with Karlo. He already had Kent and Essex pretty much under his control and was gaining a finger-hold in the East End. The Albanians already had an informal agreement to stay away from the rich pickings of the City and the West End because of the Russians there and suggested we did the same. Our manor would be West London and all points in the direction of Wales. Voytek and the Poles would be our problem, though Steve thought he could negotiate a deal here too.

Although we would use our contacts in Colombia, Morocco and Turkey to set up the drugs shipments, the Albanians would handle the drugs when they came into the country. They would then be fed into our old distribution network as well as their own. We would handle the money laundering as they wanted to steer clear of the Russians. Older people from the former Soviet Bloc had no time for them, having suffered forty-five years under Russian tyranny.

They trusted us with the money, though they made it very clear to us what would happen if any of it went missing. In exchange, they would provide soldiers for our protection, if necessary. We would need these in our battle against Voytek and the Acton Poles.

As my expertise was in money laundering, I got to know Karlo pretty well, visiting him in his home outside West

Kingsdown. Most of the Albanians took over council houses and run-down properties to stay below the radar, paying the absentee owners or council tenants well. But Karlo had broken the rules by taking over a large residential compound in the middle of the farmlands of Kent to accommodate the wife and kids that he had brought over from Tirana.

The place had been owned by a well-known criminal, but when he had gone to jail, his wife had no alternative but to sell up. Karlo was not one of those criminals who liked to throw their weight around, nor did he want to take advantage of the woman's plight. He gave her a very fair price. It was a diplomatic move. As he was making his life here, he wanted to get on well with the locals. He also made improvements to the property, adding a heated swimming pool, a tennis court and a rifle range to keep himself in practice.

It was just thirty minutes from Dover, if he had to make a rapid retreat. He also travelled home to Tirana often as he had other interests there. The house was isolated in the middle of open countryside, so it couldn't be overlooked or spied on easily and the grounds bristled with CCTV cameras. It was a mock Tudor house filled with shag-pile carpets and faux *fin de siècle* furniture. In the bathroom, there were gold taps and a gold handle on the loo, like he was some downmarket Donald Trump. Very much not to my taste, or rather to Vittoria's taste, as she made all the decorating decisions in our house.

The house was also well supplied with weapons, locked away in a secure armoury. The last thing he wanted was for his kids to get their hands on guns. Having used them himself, in anger, he knew full well the damage they could do if mishandled. However, there was, on his desk, a solid gold knuckleduster, which he often carried around with him when he left the house. It was a relic of a bygone era of criminality. On it, there was an eagle motif, an emblem of his clan.

Instead of making large shipments of drugs contained in ingots delivered direct to English ports, the drugs were now shipped to European ports in smaller amounts between the inner and outer skin of a container. As the containers were marked for transhipment to the UK, when they arrived on the Continent, customs there took little notice. They were then brought over on trucks by ferry. We avoided the Channel Tunnel as the checks there were more thorough. At the ferry ports though, there were so many containers coming through, customs were overwhelmed. They could not check them all and, while we were still in the EU, those coming from other European Union countries were simply waved through.

If one shipment got caught, so be it. There was enough getting through that it barely made a dent in the profits. The lorry driver would not be told what he was carrying and would be well paid not to ask questions. Once the truck had left the port, it would be joined by suitably anonymous cars, watching to see if it was being followed by customs or the police. At least one of the escorting vehicles would have a sunroof so that the minders could keep an eye out for police helicopters or the specially adapted Beechcraft aircraft that were used for surveillance. These could be spotted because they had a longer wingspan than normal because of the aerials built into them. They also lowered other antennae from the belly of the plane. If overhead surveillance was spotted, it was simply a matter of leading the aircraft on a merry dance until it had to land to refuel or night fell.

With the Albanian drugs money coming in, we had to up the laundering operation. The first thing you always had to do was to get the money out of the country. Naturally, Karlo wanted the cash to be taken to Albania. From there it could be divided up into smaller amounts that could be surreptitiously deposited in accounts all across the Continent. Once in the financial system, it could be legitimately transferred back to the UK to fund other ventures, if needs be.

The answer was, as always, containers. Inch-thick bundles of notes could be stuffed in the gap between the inner and outer walls of the container. Then the main body of the container would be loaded with innocent-looking furniture, ostensibly newly manufactured for export. The sofas and armchairs were unusually shaped because they were actually made from cardboard cartons containing money. This was a technique borrowed from old-style British gangsters who used to smuggle cartons of cheap cigarettes in from Spain that way.

The lorries were in danger of being hijacked by other crime outfits, so the container would be loaded in a secluded warehouse among others painted the same colour as vehicles in the yard that left at the same time. Even the driver would not be told which one was actually carrying the cash.

There was no real difficulty smuggling the money out of England. British customs would barely give containers going out of the country the time of day. I guess they were glad to see the back of the foreign drivers. As the containers were bound for Albania, which was not part of the EU, the French, Belgian and Dutch customs officials could not be much bothered either.

And when they got to Albania, the Albanian border guards could easily be bribed. At the time, crime was arguably one of Albania's major exports. It brought much-needed money into the country. Once home, Albanian criminals were free to flaunt their wealth. They lived in large houses in gated communities or behind iron railings patrolled by guards and ferocious dogs. Even there, they were in danger of being kidnapped by other criminals and Karlo was always accompanied by a couple of bodyguards.

He invited me out to Tirana to see the operation there. His house was as gaudily decorated as his place in Kent, right down to the gold-trimmed TV. The windows were bullet-proof glass and there was a helipad on the roof. There were, of course, bundles of money everywhere. I warned him not to do that. It was much safer in an offshore account.

He kept a second family in Tirana. This was not uncommon for Albanian mobsters. They didn't want to risk their wives and children being excluded from the UK, so they stayed there until they got their citizenship. Meanwhile, back in Albania, the men wanted fun and relaxation, and it was cheap enough to maintain a mistress in some style.

Karlo drove around in a Bentley Turbo, a car he would not be seen dead in in England, just in case he was seen dead in it. He wouldn't want to attract that much attention. He also had a Learjet on a private airfield with full airport facilities outside the capital. It was one of many executive jets there, though he dared not use it to fly back and forth to England. But in Albania, it was no problem. Gangsters could fly in and out of their private airstrip without any of the usual airport restrictions or security checks. The government weren't interested as the whole place was paid for by drugs money, Karlo said. I could believe that. We were shipping a container full of money back to Albania every month, stuffed with hundreds of thousands of pounds.

In Albania, he explained, you were expected to show off. He had relatives in the police force so there was no danger of being arrested. Even if he had been fleeing some crime in the UK, there was no chance that a warrant would be issued. European Arrest Warrants didn't apply and there was little chance of extradition. As long as you spread money around, spending freely and handing out bribes, no one would bother you.

Albanian gangsters built nightclubs and casinos to wash the dirty money they had made in the UK, though it was hardly necessary. Politicians were welcome at these establishments and, usually, given VIP treatment. They even cadged lifts on private jets and were guests on the luxury yachts that the drug barons kept in the well-run marinas along the Adriatic coast, again built with the proceeds of crime.

While I was in Albania, the uneasy peace back home was broken. The British old-timers decided that enough was enough. They'd been pushed out of their old rackets while the newcomers were making millions. They had learned their lesson taking on the Eastern Europeans, so they began a money laundering enterprise that undercut the Russian gangs. The rates they were charging interested the oligarchs and other entrepreneurs in town and they began dealing with the Brits behind the backs of the Russians, who soon found out. All hell broke loose. Two British soldiers disappeared. Then a couple of Russian heavies went missing in a tit-for-tat exchange.

This spooked some of the oligarchs who began to leave for Switzerland, the Côte d'Azur or Israel, taking the muscle with them. The Brits may have won the war, but it was an empty victory as the Russians took their money with them. What was left of their money-laundering operation was small time and could be handled through the thousands of fixed odds betting terminals in bookies across the country.

Meanwhile, there was another sideline that we shared with the Albanians in Kent. They had built a workshop in a shipping container where stolen jewellery could be stripped down. The gemstones were smuggled out to Antwerp or Amsterdam where they could be sold to legitimate dealers who knew nothing of their origin. A run was made every week. The gold and silver could be melted down to conceal its origin and sold on the metal markets. The Albanians handled the bent tom (foolery) our boys brought in as well as their own. This cut out the use of local fences, which had risks of its own. There were specialist investigators who could easily track down expensive pieces if they were left intact.

In another container, there was a cutting factory. There, the compressed cocaine being smuggled in would be sieved to make a fine white powder. Using Kenwood food mixers, the cutters would blend in a couple of spoonfuls of cutting powder, usually baby laxative or bath salts. They were not yet cutting it with the opioid fentanyl as they were in the States, which makes the resulting powder much more addictive and sometimes fatal.

The result was then tested by the expert blenders, doing a line each, to check it did the job. It was important that they didn't dilute it too much. The drug had to give an instant hit, otherwise you would get a lot of dissatisfied customers who wouldn't come back for more. Repeat purchase is what the drug business is all about.

The cut cocaine was then packaged up in £20 or £40 bags, which were put in plastic shopping bags. The local distribution in Kent and Essex was handled by the scooter boys. They would head out to the surrounding towns and villages where they met their customers at pre-arranged meeting points. They would text ahead and clients would gather when they heard the whine of a scooter engine. Business would be done in a couple of minutes before the scooter boy moved on.

Our business in West London was done differently. Bags would be taken up to town but we would sell in bulk to the top boys on the local council estates. They usually took over a flat – not necessarily with the rightful occupant's permission – and sold to users from there. Customers came to them rather than the other way around.

We did employ some scooter boys for more upmarket clients. They had a phone-in service. Orders would be phoned in and we would deliver to their front door. After all, a little weed or a line of coke was practically de rigueur at a middle-class dinner party in Notting Hill or Holland Park. By this time, WhatsApp was now taking over and I guess we should look forward to the time when we can offer a fully online service.

But also around this time, our Firm began to have trouble closer to home. In Acton, Voytek and his new generation of young Poles had begun to encroach on our territory. They were completely out of control and began staging knife fights in public places simply to intimidate the locals. Shameless, they began to post on Instagram showing them with drugs, wads of cash and machetes and zombie knives. This was a danger to all of us as it was bound to interest the police.

Under our agreement, the Albanians came to our assist-ance. A bunch of them came up to town with the intention of kidnapping some of the Poles. They wanted to cut off a finger or two to teach the Poles a lesson and stop them boasting on social media so we could get on with business as usual. But when three of their people were snatched off the streets of Shepherd's Bush, the Poles came back with guns blazing.

The problem with this particular influx of young Poles was that they had started using. They were so strung out on their own drugs that they didn't think through the consequences of an all-out gang war. They staged a raid on the Albanians' heartland in Kent and a number of soldiers on both sides went missing. Again, the Poles mistakenly thought that if it was just a matter of Eastern Europeans doing each other in, the cops would not take an interest. However, the fighting was so ferocious that there was always a danger that some innocent bystander might get hurt or killed and so, sure enough, there were police raids.

After this, Karlo contacted Voytek. They had a meeting and hammered out a peace deal. I had a feeling that this was not going to hold. The Poles had no particular beef with the Albanians. They were not rivals over the same territory. But Voytek had got a bit big for his boots. It was our manor he was really after.

There was little Steve could do about it. He had been ill for some time. He had been suffering from gallstones and had been in hospital to have his gall bladder removed. Then he was recuperating at home. It would be a couple of weeks before he was back up to speed. Without Mick as well, we were not in a position to organise a concerted counter-attack, but the boys were doing their best to hold their ground. People saw us as a weak link in the chain, and we knew it.

Then came the decisive blow. Steve collapsed in his garden. An ambulance had been called. A paramedic had tried to revive him, but he was dead. His shirt was soaked in blood. The emergency services thought that it had come from the keyhole surgery and that the small incision made to remove the gall bladder had opened up. Or at least that was what it looked like.

Still it was a puzzle. Apart from the problem with his gall-stones, Steve had been fit and healthy. All surgery carries a certain amount of risk, but the removal of the gall bladder is a standard procedure. That Steve should die from a minor operation was a shock. Especially for me. It changed every-thing. With Steve dead and Mick in jail, I was now in charge. Like it or not, I had become a mob boss.

# CHAPTER THIRTY-TWO
## MURDER

I went down to Dartford to offer what comfort I could to Steve's family and help organise the funeral. As one of the executors of Steve's will, there were other matters I needed to attend to. That took me away from our base. That was when the Poles made fresh attacks on our operations. It was only later that I understood why.

As Steve wasn't in hospital at the time he died and there was no immediately discernible cause of death, there had to be a post-mortem. Then came another shock. When the pathologist cut him open, they discovered that Steve hadn't died of natural causes. He had been stabbed four times with a sharp needle. The paramedic had mistaken the small wounds for the signs of surgery. Perhaps this was forgivable as there were no exit wounds. Clearly he had been killed by a professional assassin.

Mick was furious when he heard the news. He would not be allowed out to attend the funeral because the police were sure that he would try and escape to take revenge on whoever had done it. They said they had no idea who the culprit was.

We didn't know who the assassin was either, but it was

clear that Voytek must be behind it. Steve's son was also determined to go after him. I told him that his father wouldn't have gone about it that way. He had been a man of reason who would never have sprung into action on a mere suspicion and that he didn't go killing for killing's sake. He would have talked to Voytek and come to some accommodation with him. Approaching the matter in any other way would've been bad for business.

I spoke to Karlo who agreed with me. He was not keen to risk losing a son-in-law who was now the proud father of his grandson. As head of our family, it was now up to me to deal with the problem, he said. It was true. If I didn't do something decisive, The Firm would fall to bits.

It was true too that blood feuds were part of Albanian culture. It was an eye for an eye, if not two. But revenge was a dish better served cold. Karlo pointed out that I was an accountant, not an assassin. He knew that Voytek and I had been to school together so something could be sorted out. He would arrange a meeting, just the two of us, where we could hammer out our differences and come to some arrangement. In the meantime, he would organise a truce with the Poles.

I agreed, keeping my doubts to myself. It disturbed me that Karlo clearly knew Voytek. Had he been discussing doing business with him behind my back? If he had, at any meeting

I had with Voytek, he would be holding all the cards. I would be at a disadvantage.

Steve's funeral went off without a hitch. It was held back in the old manor. Mum was very upset, but Dad took it in his stride. For him, Steve's death was the death of a soldier. It was something you had to accept if you went into our line of work.

There was a good turnout. Members of The Firm who had been loyal followers of Steve for many years were there. They wanted action, revenge, but they had no clear idea of what form this would take – except that someone had to die. I could not see the point in mindless bloodshed. We might knock out some foot soldiers in the Polish gang, but some of our guys might die too, or get banged up, leaving us weaker than we had been before. Nevertheless, they looked to me to do something.

Dad took me aside. He warned me that, if I didn't take some decisive action, I would appear weak. Our guys wouldn't follow a weak leader and would likely end up plotting behind my back. Their own futures were based on the future of The Firm, and if The Firm looked like it was going down, they'd do everything they could to stop it. Also, Voytek would have no reason to hold back and would swallow up our territory. And I would lose Karlo's respect and with that his support. For once in my life, I had to play the hard man. It was the only way. After all, I owed my entire life to Steve, Mick, the family and The Firm.

The meeting was set up for the following week. It would be in one of the shipping containers that had been converted into a pop-up club. There would be no girls there, just Voytek and me. Security would be provided by Karlo and his men.

I didn't tell Vittoria what was happening. She would only have worried. After all, when we met, I had been a mild-mannered wannabe accountant. Now she was married to a mob boss.

On the day of the meeting with Voytek, I tried to go through my morning routine as normally as possible. However, after I dressed, I tucked my Skorpion into my belt. It wasn't very comfortable, but stripped of its foldable stock, silencer and with a short magazine, it was just like any other sidearm.

I wasn't used to carrying a gun and it made me feel self-conscious. I hoped Vittoria wouldn't notice it as I left the house. But although Karlo was billing my meeting with Voytek as a peace conference, I had no idea what was going to happen. With Voytek, would there be peace without my complete capitulation?

When I arrived at the container that Karlo had chosen for the meeting, under the shadow of the Queen Elizabeth II Bridge, Voytek was already there. He was chatting with Karlo. It made me uneasy that they were so matey. I didn't like it.

The Albanians were there in force, sporting, more or less discreetly, a range of firearms. Voytek and I had to surrender our guns before they patted us down to make sure that we weren't carrying any other concealed weapons.

Karlo shook our hands as he ushered us into the container. He told us to settle our differences so we could get back to business. After all, it was better to make money than shed blood. The door to the container clattered shut behind us.

The atmosphere was tense. Although we had been at school together, we had never been mates. Indeed, we had hardly ever been on speaking terms. He'd only left me, Curtis and Terry alone back then because of Steve and Mick's reputation. Still, he'd been a tough guy back then and his time back in Poland seemed to have added another, thicker layer to his hide.

'Come, let's solve this Polish style,' he said.

This sent a chill through me. He grabbed a bottle of vodka from behind the bar and filled two glasses.

'*Na zdrowie*,' he said, necking his in one.

Determined to keep my wits about me, I sipped cautiously on my drink.

'Pussy,' he said.

After another shot, he said: 'Your brother Steve got what was coming to him . . . Never underestimate the Poles. We have specialists who can deal with that sort of thing. They come and go. My man was back in Łódź that night. There's a flight from Gatwick.'

Looking impossibly smug, he poured himself another drink.

'And big brother Mickey is not here to look after you either,' he said, taking another slug. Mick was not around, Voytek said, because he had grassed him up. He laughed again.

'Mick was such a dumb-arse,' he said. 'He couldn't see that he'd been set up.'

I was puzzled. Voytek poured himself another shot and necked it.

'He didn't see it,' Voytek said. 'His best friend was one of ours.'

'Who do you mean?'

Voytek snorted.

'Mike stitched him up,' he said. 'He was always there at the time, but while Mick went to jail, Mike was home free.'

'Mike Janson?' I said, shocked. I didn't know the guy, but he had always been Mick's closest mate.

'Not Janson,' snorted Voytek. 'Mike Janulewicz. His dad changed his name when he stayed here after the war. A lot of Polacks did that because you dim Englishmen could not pronounce our names, or even spell them. My dad called himself Flowers. But I wasn't having it. I'm Voytek Florowski.'

Voytek couldn't help taunting me more. He said he'd done away with Mick and Steve, and I didn't have the balls to avenge this affront to my family. No Pole would have stood for that. I wasn't tough like the Polish gangsters. I was a soft book-reading Englishman who tried to hide behind the Albanians.

Downing another glass, he lit a cigarette, offering me one. I declined and he gave me that old-fashioned tough-guy look smokers give to wimps who are not hard enough to take on cancer.

'And you were a mate of that f***ing n****r.'

'Curtis?' I said. 'He's still a mate of mine now.'

Voytek sucked his teeth. Then he laid down the law. He and his gang were going to take over our territory. He was going to do business direct with Karlo. They were both hard men and understood each other. They knew the way of the world. It was a matter of evolution. Survival of the fittest. I was an accountant, a pussy, not a man at all. With me in charge, our Firm stood no chance at all.

But I was not the timorous schoolboy he had once known who had depended on my brothers to fight my battles for me. Though I had tried to stay out of the business of being a gangster, I had now spent my whole adult life in that world. People got killed, rubbed out. It was dog eat dog – or rather dog killed dog if needs be. I wasn't a punk any more. I had risen to the top.

He thought he knew me. But I knew myself more. I knew that was the moment I realised I was built for this job. I'd been training for it for decades. I had become a mob boss. And he was about to find out just how true that was.

I don't know whether it was the vodka that got my blood up, but I downed the glass.

'Ah,' said Voytek. 'At last, you've grown a pair.'

He turned away unsteadily to grab the vodka bottle. As he bent down to fill our glasses, I slipped the belt from around my waist. His back was to me. I quickly wrapped it around his neck and pulled hard. He gasped and grabbed at it, but the belt had tightened and there was no way he could get a grip on it.

'Tough enough for you now?' I asked, whispering it in his ear.

He shook his head and sank to his knees, spilling the drinks. I stuck my knee in the middle of his back and pulled even harder. He made a sickening gurgling sound. I guess that's what they call a death rattle. I felt no pity, no compunction, nothing but the edge of the leather belt cutting into my fingers.

I could feel him weaken. He relaxed as he became unconscious. I kept on pulling on the belt with all my strength until I was sure he was dead. I was now a cold-blooded killer. So cold that I felt nothing as I pushed his corpse to the floor.

He had insulted my friend, got Mick locked up for life and killed my brother. My dad had told me to be a hard man and I always worried if I was hard enough. I figured I had a long way to go to match up to Karlo or to earn the respect of my mob, but this was a start.

I grabbed the vodka bottle and doused Voytek's body with the remaining contents. Then I tore a strip off his shirt, grabbed another bottle of vodka from the bar then stuffed the cloth down its neck. With Voytek's cigarette lighter, I lit the wick of my makeshift Molotov cocktail. As I opened the door, I turned and flung it against the bar beside Voytek's dead body. The bottle smashed and the whole thing went up in flames. Was I f***ing hard enough now?

As I emerged from the door, Karlo looked surprised. He grabbed my hand, pulled me towards him and hugged me and kissed me on the cheeks.

'I knew that only one of you would come out of there,' he said.

Clearly, he did not expect it to be me.

How little he knew.

EPILOGUE

2020-PRESENT DAY

# CHAPTER THIRTY-THREE
## LIFE IN THE SUNSHINE

The incineration of Voytek gave me a certain amount of credibility, even among the Albanians. I was now seen as not a man to be messed with. Maybe they thought Voytek was still alive when I set him on fire. Karlo said I wasn't to worry about the fire damage to the club or the container. He could find enough surplus goods to set fire to in there to make a credible insurance claim. As for the remains of Voytek, they would throw whatever they could find of him in the river. But for the time being, Karlo thought it would be best if I left the country until everything died down. Steve's son, Karlo's son-in-law, could run The Firm in my absence and, under our agreement, he would send his soldiers to take care of any more trouble from the Poles.

I already had some property in North Cyprus. It seemed like a good investment at the time. I bought some land a little way out of the town of Karşiyaka for about £90,000 and built five villas on it. We did quite well out of this, so we bought some more land. We kept one apartment block for family use, but usually got so tied up in business elsewhere that we didn't make much use of it. For the moment, it would make a good bolthole.

Karlo arranged an anonymous vehicle to take me to Dover. Once I was across the Channel, another car was laid on to take me to Istanbul. From there I flew to Ercan International. When I say international, the only planes that land there come from Turkey.

I only meant to stay in Northern Cyprus for a short while, but there was always a danger that, following the example of Voytek, the Poles would decide to grass me up too. The Metropolitan Police might want to interview me, so I thought it was best I stayed where I was. On the ground, The Firm was in safe hands. There was, of course, now the tie of blood between Steve's son and Karlo. So they were tight.

My position was also secure. I knew where the bodies were buried. I had made some of the original drug deals and had set up the money-laundering operations. All the figures were in my head. So were the details of all our offshore bank accounts. Thanks to WhatsApp and encrypted emails I could run that part of the operation via the internet.

Vittoria had enjoyed Cyprus when we had visited. Of course, it was a surprise to her when I suddenly left the country without any prior warning. Up until then, her husband had always been the sure and steady type. But when Karlo told her what had happened, she was relieved that I was still alive and when we did eventually speak, she told me to stay where I was. She didn't want to risk me going to jail. I'm not sure that she didn't find it a little bit exciting that I was now a man of action.

It would be quite an upheaval for her, but she decided to join me in Cyprus. Although we were getting on a bit, Vittoria was still a romantic and Cyprus was where Venus had risen from the waves. And, of course, it had sunshine, like Spain.

Our girls were now grown up and doing well at university. They could visit us in the holidays. Otherwise, they had somewhere nice to live and I paid their tuition fees, plus a healthy allowance. They wanted for nothing and were at an age when they wanted their parents out of the way. Or at arm's length, at least.

While Vittoria would be able to fly back to Britain to see her parents, I wouldn't. And Mum and Dad wouldn't be coming to visit me. Neither of them had much time for abroad. But they had grandchildren who would visit. Mick would be a bit short of visitors, but Steve's sons made an effort. Besides, Mick was a tough nut who knew how to get on inside.

Although we were not expecting too many visitors in North Cyprus, Vittoria and I decided, if we were going to make our home there, we should move out of the holiday flat. Then I heard that someone was selling an old olive mill.

The Old Olive Mill needed a considerable amount of renovation. Then we bought another larger house whose garden backed on to ours. The owner had been a Greek Cypriot.

When the Turkish invasion came, he had gone on the roof to take pot shots at Turkish soldiers. He was killed and his wife fled to the south along with most of the other Greek Cypriots. This made doing the paperwork for the sale problematic.

After huge lawyers' bills and some baksheesh, we succeeded in buying it in the end, then we renovated the house from the basement up. Vittoria is an art lover and the place is filled with the most exquisite collection of paintings – a Rembrandt, *The Concert* by Vermeer, and a couple of Picassos. Not the real thing of course, though some mob bosses and drug barons do have them. But not to hang on the wall. They keep stolen artworks in safes in case other gangsters steal them.

The thing is, when a valuable painting gets stolen, forgers immediately get to work in the hope that they can pass off their copy as the genuine article – they even try it on with insurance companies and the original owner. Inevitably they get found out, but great forgeries circulate among the criminal fraternity, if you have the contacts.

Then came the bad news. For some time I had had stomach pains. I assumed that it was ulcers as I have lived a relatively stress-filled life. Eventually I got myself to hospital where I was diagnosed with bowel cancer. Much of my colon had to be removed. So far so good. Then the cancer came back. This time it was inoperable.

Vittoria has always been a devoted Catholic. Religion had

never bothered me much up to that point. But with her help and instruction I was baptised in St Elizabeth of Hungary Roman Catholic Church in Girne. I thought that was the best option. There was still a Greek Orthodox Church opposite our house and a mosque at the end of the street.

Thanks to Vittoria, I have now confessed my sins and made my peace with God. That is why she has encouraged me to write this book, seeing it as part of my confession and my penance. Otherwise, I spend my time learning a bit of Turkish and playing cricket. Some of the British Army guys who had been stationed here came back to retire in the sunshine and there is a new contingent of young Indians and Pakistanis who have come over to work in the hotels.

Anyway it was a comfort to have a bit of the Old Country here. I made the best of it. I'm not about to get on a plane back to Blighty just to taste a pint of warm beer like Ronnie Biggs did, then spend the rest of my days – or most of them – in jail. All those years ago, when visiting Dad in the Scrubs, I swore that would never happen to me.

Otherwise, I keep myself busy. I have an office upstairs in the house where I am writing this and, an hour or so every day, I attend to business. As I'm still the boss, it is my duty to the family and our mob. However, when I die, I don't want my daughters involved. They've never really known what I have done. Like their mother, they don't ask as they really don't want to know. They will surely have a flourishing career of their own choosing. When I die, they and their mother will inherit the houses in Notting Hill and Cyprus, along with other assets that I am attempting to make above board, but I suppose they will still be tainted as they come from the proceeds of crime.

I suppose wanting to keep my daughters out of The Firm would be considered sexist these days. Indeed, in Italy there have been some formidable women mob bosses. But Steve's eldest son is keen to take over and introduce some younger blood from the new generation he's grown up around in Kent and South East London. After all, he has his father-in-law to give him guidance. Steve's younger son? I'm not sure. I hope he finds his own way and is not dragged into the business the way I was.

There is still Mum and Dad to look after. I send them money regularly and see their every need is taken care off. It looks like they are going to outlive me, which is sad in its way. And I have to make provision for Mick for when he gets out, if ever. There's never been any danger of him being repentant, as least not repentant enough to impress a parole board, so he will probably have to serve his entire sentence.

It would have been nice for him to spend his remaining years in the sunshine in Spain, or here where we have a spare house. It would be easier to keep funds for him secure from the grasping hands of the authorities. But I am sure he would never be allowed to have a passport.

All that means I am still in the driving seat. Although Steve's son is running things on the ground, I am still the boss. And I'm not done yet. There's a whole heap of fresh opportunities out here – drugs, guns, organised crime, money laundering. Some of the local gangsters are planning to pop across the border to do a bank job in Nicosia. Maybe I should have a go – go out in a blaze of glory that would have made Steve and Mick proud.